SUBMIT EVERYONE

The Guerrilla Jiu-Jitsu Files

Top Secret Tactics for Becoming a Submission-Focused Fighter

Dave Camarillo
and Kevin Howell

Victory Belt Publishing
Las Vegas

Dedication

This book has been five years in the making. As you will see, Submit Everyone *is less about technique and more about acquiring the mindset to finish your opponent on the mats. This is obviously not an easy task, which is why I teamed up with Kevin Howell to write this book. Together we worked to create a book I am extremely proud of, and I hope you enjoy reading it as much as I enjoyed writing it.*

I dedicate this book to my friends and family….

To my mother Linda and my father James. My favorite thing in life is dinner at your house, talking about good times.

To my brother, Daniel. You are truly the arm-hunter. You have the best arm locks I have ever seen. I loved being on the receiving end of them for so many years.

To my wife, Shumei. Without you I would be lost. You are an enormous part of my life and Guerrilla Jiu-Jitsu. I love you.

I want to thank my Chinese mother, "Ahye." Thank you for being there. Your support has a huge impact in my life.

Without my family in my life, there would be no Guerrilla Jiu-Jitsu.

I'd like to acknowledge one of the biggest influences in my martial arts career. He's a person who has guided me when things were up and down. He has contributed to Guerrilla Jiu-Jitsu more than any other. He's a good friend and mentor. Thank you Klint Klaas.

Matt Darcy is one of my best students, one of my best instructors, and one of the most technical BJJ teachers I've ever seen. You are a huge part of Guerrilla Jiu-Jitsu and I thank you for your dedication and honor.

And to my two best friends, Peter and Taree. Even though you guys live so far away, the impact you've had on my life has been very special to me. Thank you.

I would like to end by thanking the most influential people who have helped me with my BJJ game: BJ Penn, Flavio Canto, Marcelo Garcia, and Paul Schreiner.

-Dave Camarillo

As for thanks—I cannot tell you all how gracious I am to the jiu-jitsu community and readership that purchases these books. Without all of you, our team of writers would be unable to pursue our passion for writing about the martial arts. Thank you all.

I would also like to thank my wife Haley, the unsung hero of all of my work. She works tirelessly to contribute, edit, and design all of my books and has been there for every single photo shoot, late meal, and brainstorming session. I love you Haley!

Haley and I would like to dedicate this book, as with all of my books, to our family, in particular, our two small boys—Ollie and Milo.

Boys, what you choose in life is your decision. We only hope that you pursue this life, and everything in it, with extreme passion. You two have been the pinnacle of our lives and we love you both more than words can tell.

-Kevin Howell

CONTENTS

FOREWORD by TIM FERRISS

#1 *New York Times* bestselling author of *The 4-Hour Workweek* and *The 4-Hour Body*

In your hands, you hold a manual unlike any other.

It offers the solution to perhaps *the* biggest problem in jiu-jitsu.

I'm sure you've seen it yourself: Even world-famous black belts, often world-class athletes, teach a hodgepodge of random techniques. Daily classes are submissions *du jour*, however well intentioned, that leave students to assemble the puzzle for themselves. Some succeed, the vast majority fail, and—at best—students plateau for months or years at a time.

There is no system, there is no clear progression, there is no consistency.

My first visit to AKA to train with Dave was uniquely memorable. Not because his technical abilities are amazing (which they are), not because elite judoka fear him on the ground and top jiu-jitsu players fear him on his feet (both true), but because his students were uniformly difficult to deal with.

Forget about the *UFC* champions and soon-to-be champions, both of whom travel from around the world to be engineered by the Camarillo machine and magic touch of AKA.

I found the lesser mortals to be even more impressive.

Blue belts, with far less experience that me, were throwing armbars from angles I'd never seen, and exhausting me from postures I couldn't break. At first, I assumed it was one or two outliers. No such luck. I began to see patterns—first principles—that his disciples had wired into their DNA, like Marines reassembling guns blindfolded. The positions were the same, pressure was applied in the same places, each input paired with its desired output. The 230-pound guys weren't brute forcing things like I expected—they were attempting to fine-tune in the same way that the 130-pound players had to. Something here was very different.

His students were infuriatingly *reliable*.

Over the course of the next year, I had the good fortune to live with Dave and observe his uncommon thinking firsthand. Part of the reason I moved to San Jose was to be closer to his unique brand of teaching, to be part of the laboratory. I've never had faster progress in my ground game.

This is the book I always wanted him to write, and you can count yourself lucky.

These pages will save you years of effort and frustration, and I'm glad as hell that I won't be rolling with you. Getting my ass kicked by Dave for a few photo shoots was enough to remind me of how potent his medicine can be.

May you infuriate your opponents and smile as you do it.

AUTHOR'S NOTE

It's finally here!

When I was approached to work with Dave Camarillo on the follow-up to his debut, *Guerrilla Jiu-Jitsu*, I had to think for about two seconds before responding with a resounding "yes." Little did I know that this project would be years in the making and I would finish two books that were signed after Dave's before even completing the manuscript! The reasons are many and varied, but I can honestly say that this book has been a labor of love for both of us. I have come to know the pleasure and intensity of working with Dave and have come to know him as a supremely dedicated and focused martial artist. He is a perfectionist at heart, and this is a characteristic that I quite admire.

Well, after constant writing, several trashed manuscripts, and countless revisions, it is here. It may or may not ever scratch the *New York Times* Bestseller List (I always like to aim for stars), but that is beside the point. This is the product of hard work and dedication, and it is the book that I am most proud to have finished. It is a creative, fun, and, most important, informative study of Dave Camarillo's Guerrilla fighting system. Dave and I took on a very complex and difficult subject matter and have tried to distill it into something more accessible. We made a book that teaches people how to become what we all want to be: submission fighters.

Becoming a submission-focused grappler is something that is important to me, and it has been since I was thirteen years old. Most kids like to wrestle and roughhouse, and I was no different. I still remember my old friend Mark Brazney pinning me to my back and making me say "uncle" by digging his chin into my rib cage. I would get so mad that I couldn't do anything to stop it, and all I wanted to do was make him say "uncle" instead. I remember we'd go surfing every day after school and afterward we'd go back to Mark's house where all of us would get into these little wrestling wars. Being the smallest, I was mostly on the losing end, especially seeing as Mark's uncle had taught him some real wrestling from his days as a competitor, but in the end it didn't matter. I loved the idea of the submission—the finish—and I still do.

So who better to write a book on submission fighting than Dave Camarillo? Camarillo's overriding strategy has always been to hunt for arms and go for the finish, disregarding points, and because of this he will always be a handful for any opponent, of any size or skill level. For me, this is the real essence of grappling, as again, my first exposure to wrestling was saying "uncle" on my buddy's carpet.

With this said, I hope you all find what I was looking for at age thirteen: the ability to **SUBMIT EVERYONE** regardless of skill or size. Here's to making them all say "Uncle!"

Kevin Howell

THIS CASE ORIGINATED AT   Pleasanton, CA, Guerrilla Jiu-Jitsu HQ

REPORT MADE AT:	DATE WHEN MADE:	PERIOD FOR WHICH MADE:	REPORT MADE BY:
Tracy, CA	Oct. 1, 2011	Ongoing	Kevin Howell

TITLE:	REFERENCE:
GUERRILLA JIU-JITSU TACTICS: HOW TO SUBMIT ANYONE	Report & Surveillance of David Camarillo, dated San Jose, CA Nov 15, 2008

SYNOPSIS OF FACTS:

On Nov 15, 2008, intense scrutiny and surveillance was established regarding the training methods and skill development of "Guerrilla Jiu-Jitsu" black belt and MMA instructor, SUBJECT CAMARILLO, DAVID. As of Oct. 1, 2011, Camarillo has been completely willing and forthcoming regarding this agency's investigation of the implementation of submissions as a fighting strategy and his development of better submission-focused fighters in all avenues of the grappling arts.

Following standard agency protocol, this report analyzes how Camarillo has infused his grappling forte with the classic and modern tactics and strategies of guerrilla warfare—securing the most vital area of tactical importance: the submission. Upon completion of this report, all outside agencies should have a firm understanding of how Camarillo has layered his unique submission system. This report defines the importance of submissions; introduces guerrilla tactics as a building block of submission fighting; demonstrates how fire bases are developed and serve as a strong platform of attack; explains the preparation of a strong attacking arm, or fire team; and details sensitivity development and testing, skirmishing or advanced guerrilla tactics, and the use of psychological operations for achieving a submission outcome.

The goal of report 1209-83-68-888 is to provide all current and future grappling agents with mental and technical insight into developing a submission-focused strategy for ground fighting. This pertains to both junior and senior agents (regardless of grappling background) as well as those so far unsuccessful with attaining and completing submissions for varying positions.

APPROVED AND FORWARDED:			
Erich Krauss SPECIAL AGENT IN CHARGE		1209-83-68-888 Page 1 of 2	RECORDED AND INDEXED: OCT 01 2011
COPIES OF THIS REPORT FURNISHED TO: 3- Bureau 3- Auberry		BUREAU OF INVESTIGATION OCT 01 2011 A.M. DEPARTMENT OF JUSTICE	CHECKED OFF: OCT 05 2011
		ROUTED TO: Div. One / PER:	JACKETED: / SPECIAL:

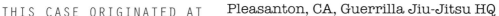

THIS CASE ORIGINATED AT **Pleasanton, CA, Guerrilla Jiu-Jitsu HQ**

REPORT MADE AT:	DATE WHEN MADE:	PERIOD FOR WHICH MADE:	REPORT MADE BY:
Tracy, CA	Oct. 1, 2011	Ongoing	Kevin Howell

TITLE:	REFERENCE:
GUERRILLA JIU-JITSU TACTICS: HOW TO SUBMIT ANYONE	Report & Surveillance of David Camarillo, dated San Jose, CA Nov 15, 2008

USING THIS REPORT:

(Continued from Page 1)

(1) This report makes strong use of SITUATIONAL REPORTS (SIT-REPs) to provide examples of the submission strategy and grappling concepts of SUBJECT CAMARILLO, DAVID. These SITREPs are the empirical support for Camarillo's assertion that anyone can become a submission-focused fighter and that these concepts can be used by any type of grappler, regardless of size, weight, skill, or grappling experience. Most agents should take these SITREPs as important lessons that can be bridged into their own particular submission game plans.

(2) While the SITREP of every technique often refers to the concept behind submission fighting, the Plan of Attack (POA) addresses the individual technique itself. In this way, the agent grappler can learn the key details of the particular movement within the SITREP itself. To help with the reprogramming of all agent brainwaves, the technique is shown in its entirety before being broken down at its most important segments during the POA.

(3) Following every SITREP is both a SNAFU moment and an AFTER-ACTION REPORT.

(3a) The SNAFU (Situation Normal All Messed Up) refers to Murphy's Law—what can go wrong will go wrong, and is included to provide all agent grapplers with answers to "what-if" problems accompanying the particular technique provided in the POA. This should serve each grappler well as he or she fleshes out his or her grappling and serves as a great jumping-off point for troubleshooting.

(3b) The AFTER-ACTION REPORT links the most important elements of the SITREP's grappling concept and directly bridges it to the individual POA. There are some very important lessons here that go far beyond lesson recaps. Agents are advised to read each carefully and apply them to their own training.

APPROVED AND FORWARDED:				RECORDED AND INDEXED:
Erich Krauss SPECIAL AGENT IN CHARGE		1209-83-68-888 Page 2 of 2		OCT 01 2011
COPIES OF THIS REPORT FURNISHED TO:	3- Bureau 3- Auberry	BUREAU OF INVESTIGATION OCT 01 2011 A.M. DEPARTMENT OF JUSTICE		CHECKED OFF: OCT 05 2011
				JACKETED:
		ROUTED TO: Div. One	PER:	SPECIAL:

CONFIDENTIAL INFORMATION

1 209-83-68-888

The Importance of Submissions

FILE 001: THE IMPORTANCE OF SUBMISSIONS

For the guerrilla, the focus in jiu-jitsu is always on the end game: submission finishes. In MMA fighting, this is the knockout or submission and for grappling arts it is the choke or lock. It is and always will be the definitive answer—total victory. It is the death on the battlefield and it is the resounding win. This will forever be the case in any art where submissions are in play.

If a practitioner in jiu-jitsu, submission wrestling, or MMA is struggling with submissions, he should first analyze the inherent weaknesses of fighting without finishes and the great advantages that are created through guerrilla-style submission training. Aside from the obvious benefit of ending the fight, the submission artist also learns transitions as his attacks and submission chains are built and fail.

Through failure he will learn to defend and escape back to submission-specific positions. As this defense grows, so will the submission ratio, because the defender learns to become comfortable with failed attempts.

In summary, the fighter who is comfortable with attacking will attack. The fighter who is not afraid of defending and escaping after a failed submission will also attack. The fighter who fears failure and never develops this necessary approach is likely to fall short both offensively and defensively in jiu-jitsu. The submission, therefore, becomes everything in guerrilla jiu-jitsu.

SECTION ONE: Points vs. Submissions

Points win tournaments, and submissions win tournaments and everything else. Though point jiu-jitsu fighters are certainly competent, they often tend to have problems as they transition from sport-specific jiu-jitsu competition to other martial arts such as submission wrestling and MMA as well as general self-defense. This is due to too much importance being placed on the point structure of particular tournaments.

This is an important lesson that guerrillas learn early: Points are sport-specific, whereas submissions cross many grappling arts. A master guard passer who can only pass but never submit may find his guard passing matters very little in MMA or other grappling events. He needs to be capable of finishing the fight and pushing the match toward the definitive victory.

SITREP 1.0 - BEATING THE ESCAPE - THE POINTS STRATEGY

SITREP 1.0 displays a correct jiu-jitsu movement that keeps an attacker at an advantage, but does not actively pursue the fight-ending submission, making this an obvious points-style strategy. This is an excellent transition that counters the opponent's near-side hip escape and certainly has guerrilla elements in that the technique does not end in a lost position or the opponent's successful counter or escape. In this regard, this is an excellent example of a technical transition that is perfectly suitable for jiu-jitsu tournaments and points-oriented strategies. By following this approach, the attacker does not lose top position, gains important transition skills, and still has the possibility of taking the back, side control, or attaining the finish. However, he misses the opportunity to conserve energy by finishing the fight with overwhelming offense as in SITREP 1.1, and has left open a chance for success in his opponent's path of escape (POE).

Plan of Attack:

a. Beginning from a previously secured side control position, the defender, CONTACT: DARCY, MATTHEW is aggressively escaping his hips away from SUBJECT: CAMARILLO, DAVID. Camarillo senses the transition long before Darcy's hips have escaped by feeling his left shoulder lift from the mat. This first indicator tells the guerrilla fighter to secure Darcy's left arm with an underhooking right arm and to pressure into the shoulder to slow the escapee.

b. Pressure on the shoulder alone cannot prohibit a strong subject like Darcy from escaping his hips or rising to his knees. Camarillo realizes this and steps over the head and secures Darcy's arm with his left arm to secure the back. This arm control is the single-minded goal of Camarillo as soon as he departs side control with shoulder pressure.

c. To finish the transition, Camarillo continues his transition toward Darcy's hips as he removes his right arm from his arm-hugging grip. Camarillo will then grab either an over-and-under control or both arms under the armpits grip. As long as the subject keeps his hips behind Darcy's arms and his weight on his hips, he will keep control of the turtle and avoid the bottom SNAFU.

DO NOT ATTEMPT

SITREP 1.1 - SUBMITTING OFF THE ESCAPE - GUERRILLA ATTACK

SITREP 1.1 epitomizes the guerrilla attack game in stark comparison to SITREP 1.0. In the previous move, the attacker acts cautiously and opts for control rather than the submission. In the following movement, the guerrilla immediately attacks the rear choke to stay on the offensive. In the case of failure, this movement will lead to other immediate submission opportunities such as the kimura or armbar (SITREP 1.2), whereas failure in SITREP 1.0 will only lead to more work in passing the guard. This strategy is at the crux of submission offense.

Plan of Attack:

a. As in SITREP 1.0, SUBJECT CAMARILLO is in side control as CONTACT DARCY, MATTHEW, is trying to escape with a strong near-side hip escape. Camarillo's initial goal is to keep pressure on Darcy's left shoulder while keeping his knee pinned close to Darcy's right hip to stifle his hip movement. This buys Camarillo the time to control Darcy's left arm with his left arm and to step over Darcy's head to initiate the transition.

b. Camarillo senses that Darcy wants to continue fighting for the hip escape or possibly scramble toward his knees. To combat this, Camarillo steps around to Darcy's back in a similar fashion to SITREP 1.0. This time, the guerrilla has the attacking mindset and is already looking for a lapel choke with his right hand. Meanwhile Camarillo uses sufficient strength and positioning to thwart Darcy's movement.

c. To stabilize the position, Camarillo first flattens under Darcy's left shoulder to prevent his scooping escape. Then, he lifts Darcy's shoulder while scooting his right shin to Darcy's back to set up the back-taking maneuver. Darcy can no longer turn away or scoop his shoulders to the mat.

d. Camarillo sets up the back control by lifting Darcy's left elbow to create space to enter the belt line hook—Camarillo's controlling left leg. Throughout the transition, Camarillo never lets up on the choke as he continues to tighten the submission. This diverts Darcy's attention away from the back control.

e. The rear choke is finalized as Camarillo steps over Darcy's right shoulder, trapping his right arm and eliminating its defense. Camarillo finishes by crossing his legs to secure the control while pulling his body to a perpendicular angle to finish the attack with a great torquing movement and a strong pull on the lapel.

SNAFU MOMENT:

If the lapel is lost in the early transition to the back, secure an over-and-under wrestler's grip and continue with the plan of attack. It is vital that the attack is continued and momentum remains with the guerrilla. The submission can be attacked once more as the belt line hook is attained. If the contact manages to escape the choke once the belt line hook is achieved, immediately transition to the kimura and armbar attack game as discussed in SITREP 1.2. Regardless of the SNAFU, continue forward with the attack in this SITUATION.

AFTER-ACTION REPORT:

Both SITREP 1.0 and 1.1 counter the opponent's path of escape (POE)—the hip escape away from the attacker's side control position. However, both SITREPs are not equal. SITREP 1.1 focuses on submissions to stay on the attack and to keep the opponent mentally and physically defensive. All counters lead to further submission attempts. SITREP 1.0 is a strong strategy and is conducive to point tournaments and for those without the mental, technical, and physical assets to push forward with the guerrilla attack. The recommendation is to stay focused on physical conditioning, attacking coordination, and fighting spirit to further develop the 1.1 offensive.

SITREP 1.2 - CHOKE OFF DEFENSE - THE IMPORTANCE OF PREPARATION

   Whenever a guerrilla sets in on an attack, preparation becomes the determinant of successful submission hunting. SITREP 1.2 successfully feeds off the attacking style of SITREP 1.1. Once in the attacking position for the choke, it is imperative that the guerrilla attacker stays focused on finishing the fight and preparation for all possible contingencies. At this point, the attacker is in what is called an end-game scenario, where all possible defenses should lead to another submission. From here, the control should only be used to benefit the choke, the ude garame kimura lock, and juji gatame armlock as the attacker pursues the end game. Uncertainty in the POA (plan of attack) can lead to failure, so the guerrilla must ensure total awareness of submission combinations prior to situational realization. Remember the military adage of the 7 Ps: Proper Planning and Preparation Prevents Piss Poor Performance.

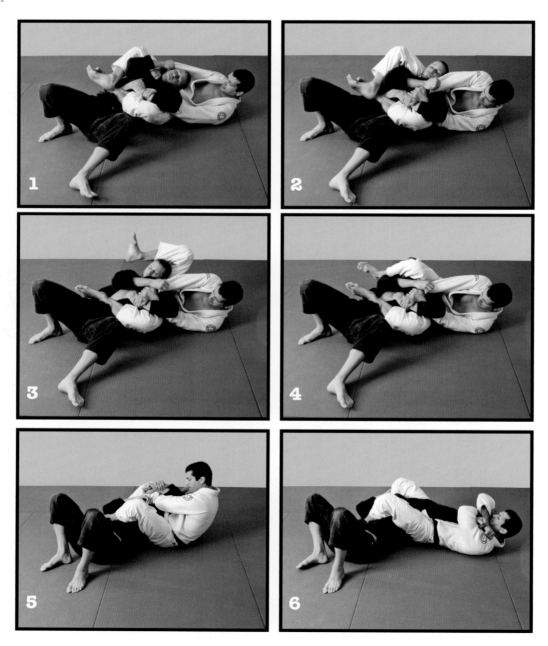

Plan of Attack:

a. In this scenario, CONTACT DARCY, MATTHEW, is successfully defending the rear choke by pulling SUBJECT CAMARILLO's choking arm over his head. Instead of fighting for a lost submission, Camarillo transitions to a figure-four control on Darcy's left arm. To prevent Darcy from sitting up, Camarillo pressures his right elbow into Darcy's head while he drives Darcy's left arm into his chest to block his progress.

b. With Darcy's upward mobility limited due to the figure-four control, Camarillo easily crosses his right leg over as he moves into the standard juji gatame position. Note that Camarillo does not relent on the pressure from the figure-four lock as he transitions to the next submission.

c. To effect the armlock, Camarillo needs to put Darcy's back on the floor. Otherwise, he risks an escape into the guard as he falls back into the submission. The guerrilla simply pushes down on Darcy's head with his right leg while keeping both legs heavy to move Darcy into an attackable position.

d. The millisecond Darcy's shoulders hit the ground, Camarillo explodes backward into the armbar position. He makes sure to squeeze his knees together, hug Darcy's wrist, and drive his hips upward while keeping Darcy's wrist vertical for the submission.

SNAFU MOMENT:

If the opponent blocks the leg over the head in the transition to the armbar, there are some strong options for the attacker: attack the kimura for the finish or transition to the back and attack the choke. If the opponent rolls, both the kimura and omoplata are viable options, and if he drives forward, the closed guard armbar game should immediately be applied. Once more, the focus should be on staying with submission-focused attacks.

AFTER-ACTION REPORT:

By staying with the attack and focusing on the relationship between end-game submissions, the guerrilla is able to create the sensation that he is too far ahead of his opponent and that the lead is insurmountable. Regarding skill acquisition, there should be a focus on basic submissions and their interrelation to produce the necessary speed and timing. For SITREP 1.2 in particular, the ude garame kimura grip was the controlling hub that allowed for seamless transition between the back and the armbar, as well as other submission avenues.

SITREP 1.3 - MOUNT AND ATTACK - WHEN POINTS ARE NECESSARY

Staying on the attack is crucial for guerrillas, but there is a time when the attacker has to improve his position to stay on the attack. This is where point fighting meets submission attacking for the benefit of the guerrilla's future attacks. SITREP 1.3 showcases a strategy against an overly defensive and physically strong opponent. Instead of forcing a submission that is not present, it is best to pursue a better position. As always, it is key to attack in the transition and always to be prepared for the slightest opening. In this situation, as soon as the elbow opens, attack the head-and-arm triangle choke.

Plan of Attack:

a. SITREP 1.3 opens with SUBJECT CAMARILLO attacking the back position of CONTACT DARCY, MATTHEW. Darcy is swimming his arms underneath Camarillo's over-and-under control to escape the possible choking technique. At this point, Darcy is using his strength to keep his elbows locked down to avoid any arm submissions while he opens his legs in base for the escape.

b. Once his right arm breaks free of Camarillo's grip, Darcy bridges off the mat to push his shoulders to the floor. With his elbows firmly locked inward, Camarillo must grip Darcy's left elbow to retain control of the situation.

c. Camarillo controls the transition by sitting up on his elbow and stiff-arming Darcy's elbow toward his head. As he does this, he makes a bridging movement of his own—this time to drive his hips into the mounted position.

d. Camarillo's stiff-arm and bridge have opened a gap under Darcy's arm, and he immediately capitalizes on it. Camarillo swims under the elbow and locks his arm around Darcy's head with his elbow on the mat. It is important that Camarillo pressures his weight into Darcy's triceps to control the submission. From here, he can attack head-and-arm triangles or continue to arm locks or back submissions.

SNAFU MOMENT:

If the opponent does not open his elbows as he is stiff-armed, likely due to a large discrepancy in strength, transition instead to either the mount or side control on top (using a hook kick over). Whenever an opponent dedicates himself entirely to a tight elbow defense, he leaves himself available to transitions to other positions such as the mount. If the opponent moves to defend the mounting action at any time, use that moment to trap an arm or elbow and go back on the attack.

AFTER-ACTION REPORT:

The difference between SITREP 1.0 and SITREP 1.3 is startling. Where SITREP 1.0 adopts a conservative mindset to stay in control of the match, it gives up a possible submission due to hesitation. SITREP 1.3 focuses on a guerrilla-minded individual who wants to submit but cannot based on current position and strength. It is because of this relationship between position and strength that the guerrilla can easily transition to the top where he will resume attacking in earnest.

SECTION TWO: Submissions as Offensive Strategy

Guerrillas always want their opponents to be reactionary instead of progressive. A reactionary opponent is overwhelmed, mentally fatigued, frustrated, and late. A progressive opponent is in control of the match and is shaping the pace and direction.

Therefore, it is of extreme importance that the guerrilla uses repeated submission attacks to stay ahead of the fight; to force the opponent, regardless of skill, to become reactionary. This cannot be emphasized enough: a guerrilla needs only to attack one more time than the opponent's last defensive maneuver; if the opponent defends three times, the guerrilla must attack four. If he gives up on the attack too early, all of the previous work may be for naught and he may face a reinvigorated opponent who is more than ready to press an attack of his own.

This ideal applies in both advantageous and disadvantageous positions. In a positive situation, a guard player may attack a submission series five times before he lands the proper submission. On the negative side, a guerrilla on the bottom of a sprawl may use offensive moves from odd positions to either force a reversal or move into a fight-winning submission. Regardless of the origin, the submission is the strongest and most feared weapon in the arsenal and it should be the first, second, and third line of approach.

SITREP 1.4 - LEARNING TO ATTACK CONTINUOUSLY

SITREP 1.4 is a guerrilla showcase. This trainable scenario is driven by the purpose of staying active and offensive with submissions without end to win the fight. A guerrilla has to be prepared to attack continuously until the attack is fruitful, and he should understand that if his opponent defends with 100 escapes, he needs to always be ready to attack 101 submissions. Guerrillas do not accept escape or fall back into a game of trading positions with up-and-down fights. Stay offensive and stay ahead.

Plan of Attack:

a. SUBJECT CAMARILLO is in a no-gi situation attempting a juji gatame armlock against CONTACT FERRISS, TIMOTHY. Camarillo takes an S-mount with his right leg so that he can de-weight and easily swing his left leg over Ferriss's head for the arm attack. His grips are in place to attack Ferriss's right arm.

b. Utilizing excellent mat sensitivity and timing aided by the gi-less slip factor, Ferriss is able to turn away from the attack and scramble to his knees. Camarillo feels the turn and goes with Ferriss's momentum as he crosses over to Ferriss's right side.

c. As soon as Ferriss arrives in the turtle, he is already too late. Camarillo is on top and has slid his right foot inside to make a back hook. Camarillo then plants his right hand on the mat to anchor and balance himself while he grips under Ferriss's left arm for control.

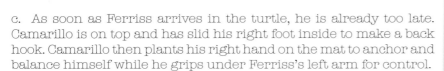

d. Camarillo continues by pushing off the mat and throwing his left knee to Ferriss's left inside hip. This propels Ferriss into a left side roll.

e. SUBJECT Camarillo rides the momentum of the roll all the way until he terminates on his right hip. With his bottom hook still in place, Camarillo locks his legs and immediately attacks Ferriss's neck.

f. Ferriss does not give up and await the choke. Instead, he opens his left leg and tries to hurdle Camarillo's unhooked left leg. Camarillo understands this risk and has prepared himself. He opens his left hook to "catch" Ferriss's leg before his left hip lands clear to the mat.

g. Ferriss lands with his back taken with both hooks. Still, the guerrilla fighter does not rest, he is on the wrong side to attack a clean choke with his right arm, and he can already feel that Ferriss is clamping down on his left arm to prevent the full rear naked choke.

h. As Ferriss continues to clamp down on Camarillo's left arm in defense, Camarillo secures a figure-four lock on Ferriss's left arm and slides his left leg into a belt-line hook across his abdomen, not unlike SITREP 1.2. As with 1.2, Camarillo keeps his right elbow heavy while he drives Ferriss's left arm into him for full body control.

i. Already on the attack, Camarillo does not waste time and immediately steps his right leg over Ferriss's head to set up the juji gatame armlock and ude garame kimura series. By changing to a belt-line hook, Camarillo has ensured that Ferriss cannot power forward into a top half-guard situation.

j. The positioning is nearly finished. Camarillo drives his legs down to push Ferriss onto his back. Both his legs are now in command of Ferriss's entire torso while his figure-four lock continues to assist in body control. Still, it will take too much power for Camarillo to pull Ferriss's arm free from this position, so he continues forward.

k. To free the arm, Camarillo sits forward and secures Ferriss's left triceps to his body and slides his left arm deep in a rear-naked-like control of the biceps.

l. Now, when Camarillo falls back into the armbar, the weight and force of his entire body easily pull Ferriss's arm free from its defensive posture. Camarillo finishes strong by driving his hips upward while his feet push toward the floor. To control the arm, he pinches his knees and keeps Ferriss's wrist vertical for the tight finish.

SNAFU MOMENT - DEPEND ON MURPHY'S LAW:

Every moment of SITREP 1.4 is a study in Murphy's Law. What can go wrong, will go wrong—always. The defending opponent will always keep defending, otherwise he is finished. This should be expected, and that is why it is important to stay progressive with attacks. The second the attacks abate, a determined defender will escape—after all, this is often the best option for the defender, and this must be realized.

AFTER-ACTION REPORT:

Through complex and continuous submission flow training and drilling, the guerrilla fighter is able to stay focused on the attack. He does not see the finish as something that always happens immediately and is prepared to stay with the attack once he has entered into the end game. Even a slippery or strong opponent can be controlled, as long as the guerrilla does not become disheartened by the escapes and stays focused on the end.

SITREP 1.5 - ESCAPING THE BOTTOM OFFENSIVELY

In SITREP 1.5, the opponent should feel confident; he is in a stronger starting position and has possible submissions available to him. Instead, the guerrilla's submission assault has left him uncomfortable and uncertain of even the slightest chance of success.

Instead of only defending the bottom position, the guerrilla goes on a full-fledged assault of whatever is exposed. He relies on submissions as an offensive strategy, even when it comes to setting up a smart defense from an inferior position. Now the defender becomes the attacker and the opponent has to worry about two things: first, defending the submission and second, escaping the submission. Both of these factors keep him from staying on the attack or preventing the counter in the chaos.

Importance of Submissions

Plan of Attack:

a. SITREP 1.5 opens with SUBJECT CAMARILLO defending the side control pin against CONTACT FERRISS, TIMOTHY. Camarillo is facing away from Ferriss and stiff-arming his left elbow, preventing Ferriss from anchoring his weight with a cross-face control. With no way of consolidating the position, Ferriss chooses to transition into the north-south position before Camarillo can hip escape or sit up.

b. As in SITREP 1.4, Camarillo does not fight Ferriss's movement. Instead, he transitions with him and follows him to a downed position underneath. Now Camarillo has gained some mobility and has a chance to reverse the position or counter.

c. Before Ferriss can navigate all the way to the back control or attack either a turn-over or strangulation, Camarillo wraps his right arm over Ferriss's exposed left elbow and secures it in a figure-four lock. Immediately, Camarillo pulls up on Ferriss's wrist and begins driving his elbow to the mat.

d. Camarillo creates space by sliding his left leg back and then drives Ferriss into where his left leg was by cranking his elbow to the mat.

e. Without an arm to check his balance, Ferriss falls to the mat on his left side and Camarillo moves to the top control.

f. If Camarillo tries to finish from this position, he will have to rely on pure strength or an incredible weight advantage. Instead, he continues to put pressure on the elbow and shoulder and he slides his legs toward Ferriss's right side.

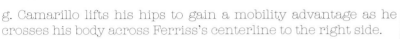

g. Camarillo lifts his hips to gain a mobility advantage as he crosses his body across Ferriss's centerline to the right side.

h. Upon arrival at Ferriss's right side control, Camarillo locks his left elbow to Ferriss's neck and attacks the Americana-style ude garame submission by sliding Ferriss's knuckles on the mat toward his own hip while lifting his elbow skyward. This pressures Ferriss's left shoulder incredibly and he is forced to submit.

SNAFU MOMENT:

If the opponent counters by moving back to the original side control, his base will be compromised and he can be easily countered with a fireman's carry-style throw. Otherwise, if the opponent escapes the figure-four while transitioning, he will still be exposed to single- and double-leg counters as well as guard recovery techniques.

AFTER-ACTION REPORT:

Part of staying aggressive in the attack throughout SITREP 1.5 is in the figure-four grip. As soon as the guerrilla locks in the control, he torques it so that it never again feels comfortable. This creates trepidation in the opponent and helps the guerrilla to escape and continue through to the finish.

Moreover, none of this would be successful without the proper elbow exposing technique of the stiff-arm. The stiff-arm is crucial for exposure and offensive control.

SECTION THREE: Moving Past the Gi vs. No-Gi Debate

The gi versus no-gi debate does not exist for guerrilla attackers; there is only grappling and submissions. If a person has excellent judo tosses, superior wrestling throws and scrambles, amazing sambo foot locks and arm attacks, and fantastic jiu-jitsu submission chains, is he a judoka/wrestler/samboist/jiujitsuka? No, he is an excellent grappler with the ability to improvise between the arts and flourish regardless of the grappling venue or style. This open-mindedness is not for talking points alone, it is essential to becoming an absolutely incredible grappler and well-rounded submission artist.

Grappling arts can be broken down for their micro elements—those that make great use of rules, uniforms, special grips, and technical elements that allow one to reach the highest levels. They can also be broken down by their macro elements—the gross motor skills that are shared between the arts and disseminate easily between different styles. Both the micro and macro skills have great cross-training benefits for other arts. For instance, the multitude of submissions available in a kimono far outweighs the number available without. This affects the kimono player by giving him a varied and rich level of defense with a greater level of tactical awareness. In this regard, the micro elements and nuances of gi training can benefit the grappling IQ of an otherwise gi-less grappler. On the other hand, without the friction of a kimono certain arm attacks and submissions are far more difficult to secure. This means a guerrilla grappler should endeavor to train his best submissions until they are tight without the kimono to ensure they are ruthlessly effective once the kimono is worn. This is a macro exchange where the gi is only used as a friction tool instead of for its more intricate techniques.

So regardless of the gi versus no-gi debate, gi-less grapplers and fighters should train in the gi for friction training (especially escaping), technical expansion, and skill broadening. Also, the kimono enthusiast should moonlight without the gi to ensure tightness, speed in scrambling, and grip exchanges that may otherwise prove unnerving. Both should seek to be one—a guerrilla grappler that has the submission in sight and steadfast determination to achieve it.

SITREP 1.6 - THE ARMDRAG - WRESTLING'S INFLUENCE

SITREP 1.6 is a great example of how grappling arts have influenced each other. In this transition that often leads to a rear naked choke, one can see what happens when jiu-jitsu positioning like the seated open guard and back positions meet freestyle and Greco-Roman wrestling's arm drag control.

Originally used as a setup for clearing the arm for single- and double-leg takedowns, now the arm drag is used to beat the guard pass and attack the back as seen in gi jiu-jitsu, submission wrestling, and mixed martial arts.

As a transition, gi practice has also benefitted from this. It is much easier for the opponent to whip out of the arm drag, and the bottom player has to use more of his body and grip to stay tight to the transition. This produces a strong control game and fast transition that helps all areas of guerrilla grappling.

Plan of Attack:

a. SUBJECT CAMARILLO begins in the seated or hooks guard with CONTACT THOMSON, JOSHUA, kneeling with both hands on Camarillo's knees, ready to pass. Camarillo is postured forward to avoid being pushed to his back and is coiled up for the arm drag reversal and back transition.

b. In one combination, Camarillo secures Thomson's wrist with his left hand and cups his triceps with his right. With the arm fastened, Camarillo kicks his left leg to the outside and drives Thomson's right arm inward.

c. With a strong pulling action, Camarillo pulls Thomson forward until he lands in a chest-to-triceps position. Meanwhile, Camarillo pulls his body to the outside and down toward Thomson's legs.

d. Having cleared Thomson's right arm, Camarillo hugs under Thomson's left arm and posts his left hand to the mat for balance and drive.

e. Finally, Camarillo drives off the mat with his right hand and opens his right knee for balance. This drives Camarillo to Thomson's back where he can continue his attack.

SNAFU MOMENT—THE WHIP OUT AND NEGATIVE STEP:

If the opponent pulls out of the arm drag before his back has been exposed, everything is okay. He will likely expend more energy escaping than attacking, and the guerrilla is still in the guard position ready for a secondary attack.

However, if the opponent tries to step backward into a negative side half guard, the guerrilla should be prepared to open his left leg (see SITREP 1.4) and secure the back in transition.

AFTER-ACTION REPORT:

By combining winning wrestling techniques like the arm drag technique, guerrilla jiu-jitsu practitioners are able to "plug in" the best grappling technique for any particular situation.

In this movement in particular, with the arm cleared, there is nothing stopping the guerrilla fighter from pouncing on the back and quite possibly the rear choke or armlock as well.

SITREP 1.7 - ARMDRAG ATTACK - WRESTLING WITH FRICTION

The comparisons between SITREP 1.6 and 1.7 are immediate and obvious. Both are arm drags and originate from the guard position, and both mesh wrestling with jiu-jitsu. However, SITREP 1.7 utilizes the friction of the kimono-to-kimono contact to set up the submission, whereas SITREP 1.6 focuses on grip and speed for success.

For training purposes, this movement is essential for gi-less and MMA-focused guerrillas. By getting the most out of the kimono's friction, the guerrilla increases his likelihood of success and can therefore work on perfecting body mechanics and technique before attempting this in a gi-less or MMA training scenario.

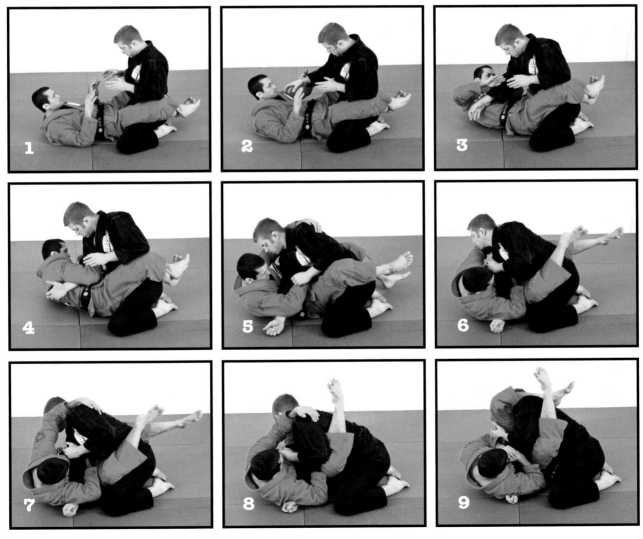

Importance of Submissions

Plan of Attack:

a. Having previously intercepted the right arm of CONTACT DARCY, MATTHEW, SUBJECT CAMARILLO has already cleared Darcy's right arm with his arm drag. Notice that the guerrilla cups the triceps, has Darcy's arm cleared all the way to his armpit, and is crunching forward to keep his arm trapped.

b. To capitalize on the armdrag, Camarillo must escape his hips outside to the left to threaten the back-take as he reaches behind Darcy to secure his left shoulder. This makes Darcy fearful of having his back taken and he will react accordingly.

c. Darcy worries about having his back taken, so he drives his body weight to the right side to block Camarillo's path of attack toward the back. Though his back is safe, Darcy has just walked into Camarillo's trap by exposing his right arm. Camarillo blocks Darcy's head with his left arm, moves his hips out and climbs his right arm high into his armpit. This pushes Camarillo into a perpendicular angle.

d. With the angle made, Camarillo's hips are in perfect alignment with Darcy's right arm. Camarillo finishes by locking his left leg over Darcy's head and driving his hips high into his armpit. Darcy will be forced to tap as Camarillo hyperextends his elbow joint by thrusting his hips upward and clamping down with his legs.

SNAFU MOMENT:

Sometimes the opponent does not respond to the guerrilla's arm attack by driving his weight against the direction of the arm drag. If this happens, simply hip escape, continue cupping either his waist or shoulder, and finish with the arm drag to the back as in SITREP 1.7. Force your opponent to give you the armbar by making the transition to the back a real threat.

AFTER-ACTION REPORT:

By attacking the arm drag and threatening the back transition, the guerrilla is able to take control of his opponent's reactions and finish with the intended submission. Again, this movement is only assisted through the practice of gi-less training in wrestling arm drags and all of their iterations.

This is not to say that training in this gi version is without merit for gi-less guerrillas. Utilizing the kimono-to-kimono friction, the guerrilla can adequately slow and control the pace of the fight, enabling him to work on his form and technique to a much higher level than he can without the gi.

Once this action-reaction sequence is mastered, it is advised that the aspiring guerrillas try to bridge this skill to gi-less and MMA training as well.

SITREP 1.8 - 1/4 NELSON - WRESTLING WITH THE KIMONO

SITREP 1.8 again expertly weaves wrestling techniques and reversals with jiu-jitsu's framework of positions. In this situation, the guerrilla uses wrestling's quarter nelson movement because it is just as effective without the kimono or in MMA.

By putting a great cranking pressure on the neck, a hallmark of competitive, folk-style, and professional wrestling, the guerrilla is able to use discomfort and head control to take advantage of one of his opponent's most vulnerable areas of attack—his back.

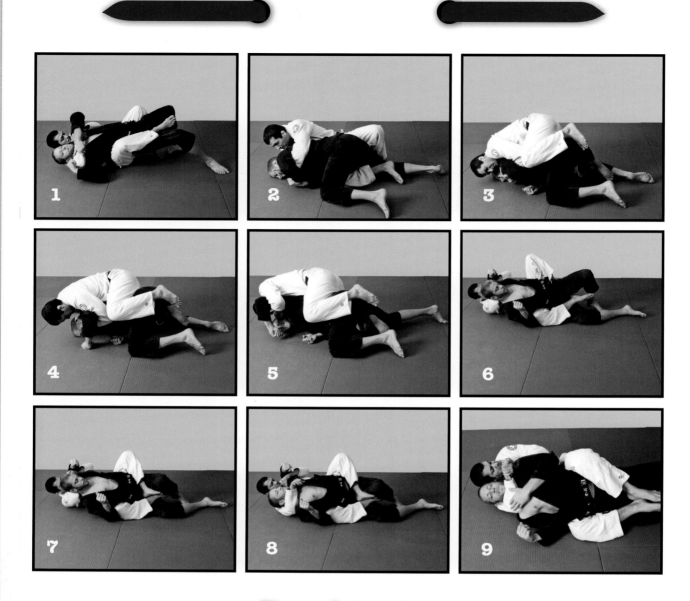

Plan of Attack:

a. SUBJECT CAMARILLO begins in the back position with the bottom hook secured on CONTACT DARCY, MATTHEW. Camarillo is correctly attacking the choke with his right arm, preventing Darcy from driving his shoulders to the mat to escape.

b. Darcy is in survival mode and turns away from Camarillo to avoid the choke. Camarillo follows using his over-and-under control to pull his body to Darcy's back.

c. As Camarillo climbs his hips onto Darcy's waistline, he releases his choking grip and slides his right forearm behind Darcy's neck and grips his left hand with a palm-to-palm grip. Once the quarter nelson is in place, Camarillo drives his forearm into Darcy's neck while he lifts his left armpit, forcing Darcy to roll to his back to avoid the neck crank.

d. Having rolled Darcy with the neck crank, Camarillo continues the prying motion to expose Darcy's left side by separating his elbow and knee defensive line.

e. In one motion, Camarillo secures the left hook and then reaches around Darcy's neck to attack the fight-ending choke. As always, Camarillo chokes with his bottom-lying arm to avoid Darcy's escape attempt.

THE IMPORTANCE OF UNDERSTANDING THE RULES:

If this movement is a part of a guerrilla's game plan, he should make sure that it is legal prior to attempting it in certain gi and gi-less jiu-jitsu events. Some tournaments may disqualify based on the neck-cranking aspect of the hold.

Not understanding the rules is not only SNAFU, but it is also FUBAR. All guerrillas should be focused on preparation in its entirety for success.

AFTER-ACTION REPORT:

Using the neck crank and quarter nelson are efficient ways to expose the back because the focus is on the head. The body always follows the head, so instead of focusing solely on areas where an opponent is strong, such as an upper leg or arm control, focus on the neck and its relative weakness to superior body control.

When it comes to the neck, don't forget to combine any quarter nelson turnover with rear naked, arm triangle, D'arce, and/or Brabo-style chokes.

SITREP 1.9 - KOUCHI GARI - USING UNORTHODOX JUDO

Though SITREPs 1.6–1.8 referred to the interrelation of different wrestling styles, jiu-jitsu, and submission wrestling, it should also be referenced that a savvy guerrilla practitioner can pull from gi-specific arts like judo for gi-less arts like submission wrestling. As a guerrilla attacker, one needs to be ready to pull the most effective attacks from the art that is best at it. For combining throws and submissions or throws and dominant positional transitions, there is no better art than judo.

In this situation, the guerrilla uses a judo-style throw to confuse and attack his opponent's defense. While most jiu-jitsu players may stalemate in this scenario as they attempt to retake the back against an opponent's strong defense and many wrestlers try a rear tackle that may be expected, this judo throw dramatically changes the angle and path of attack. This is in stark contrast to the jiu-jitsu practitioner and wrestler who would love to stay on the back control. By changing the approach and understanding a more complete view of grappling arts, the guerrilla is best suited to finding the fastest route to the finish line—the submission.

Plan of Attack:

a. SUBJECT CAMARILLO has attained the back position on CONTACT THOMSON, JOSHUA. Thomson, however, is already deftly defending the position by removing Camarillo's left hook with his left hand. If Camarillo does not act, he may lose the position as his weight pulls him off Thomson's back toward Thomson's right side.

Importance of Submissions

b. Though he has lost the back, Camarillo maintains his over-and-under grip as long as possible to avoid Thomson's counter throw or switching maneuver. Already thinking ahead, Camarillo hooks his right leg deep behind Thomson's right knee.

c. In a flash, Camarillo changes attacks. He brings his right arm over Thomson's head and hugs his left hip. This brings Camarillo's head to the floor and starts to pull Thomson toward the mat.

d. At this point, it is too late for Thomson. Camarillo puts his left hand on the floor for base and kicks his right leg skyward. Thomson has no chance to defend and immediately falls backward as his leg is reaped out from under him.

e. As Thomson smashes to the floor, Camarillo makes sure to land over his hips. From here, Camarillo has successfully countered Thomson's defense and is now in a top control position where he can launch rear strangulations and strikes to finish the match.

SNAFU MOMENT:

Luckily there are plenty of strong attacks from the back position if this fails. However, it is important to understand that unless you are of a lighter weight with good full-body strength, it may be a bad idea to jump to the back and lock your hooks over the defending arm. Unless your attack is precise and strong, you may get thrown if you are fighting a strong top-playing judoka.

AFTER-ACTION REPORT:

Surprise is an element that will be talked about in detail when it comes to guerrilla fighting. To best utilize this skill, look at the rules and standard path of progress as taught. Then look to other arts that can find a similar result through a radically different approach. That is what the kouchi gari does for the submission fighter. It confuses the opponent and provides an opportunity to progress the match in one's own favor.

SITREP 1.10 - JUJI FLIP - SAMBO'S GUERRILLA CONNECTION

The rules of the different grappling arts dictate the paths of each art's evolution. In the case of judo and Russian sambo, their rules allow for a quick standup from the downed or turtle position if progress isn't made quickly. Because chokes are limited in judo and sambo in particular and time is of the essence, both have adopted a rapid-fire approach to armbars from the turtle.

This makes these styles of attacks essential to the guerrilla's repertoire. Always looking for an element of advantage, the guerrilla uses confusing jiu-jitsu against wrestlers, wrestling neck holds against submission grapplers, and sambo and judo attack plans against traditional jiu-jitsu fighters.

Plan of Attack:

a. SUBJECT CAMARILLO is attacking the back of CONTACT DARCY, MATTHEW, and Darcy is defending the second hook as if he is fighting a strictly jiu-jitsu fighter by keeping his right knee tight to his elbow to close off space. Choking options are also limited because Darcy is keeping his hands close to his neck to block the path of the choke.

b. Understanding that the choke and hook will be difficult to attain, the guerrilla attacker switches to a sambo-style attack. Camarillo controls Darcy's left elbow with his right hand and he takes a large counterclockwise step over his head to arrive on his left side. To assist the control, Camarillo grips Darcy's belt and keeps his left hook between Darcy's legs.

c. From this setup, Camarillo sits close to his left heel, placing incredible pressure on Darcy's left shoulder. This alone forces Darcy into a forward roll.

d. To finish the sumi gaeshi reversal, Camarillo falls backward while pulling on Darcy's belt and using his own hook to propel Darcy upward.

e. As Darcy lands from the forward roll, Camarillo pulls on his belt to arrive in a perpendicular armlock position. At this point, the guerrilla finishes by hyperextending his opponent's elbow joint.

SNAFU MOMENT:

If the opponent is either strong or flexible enough to limp-arm his trapped limb out of the attack before the roll, simply continue the counterclockwise step and return to the back control or attack the inverted armbar as he tries to posture away from the attack.

AFTER-ACTION REPORT:

As with the previous SITREPs, a great guerrilla fighter must have variety in his attack game if he is to be successful against different styles of grappling. If a guard player only fights guard players, it is highly unlikely he will develop a strong top game to submission game, whereas if he learns to attack in all aspects of grappling, he is likely to be a capable fighter wherever the fight takes him and regardless of the grappling style that he may face.

CONFIDENTIAL INFORMATION

1209-83-68-888

Introduction to Guerrilla Tactics

FILE 002: INTRODUCTION TO GUERRILLA TACTICS

Guerrilla tactics revolve around three basic building blocks: —(1) core submissions, those that can be trained at full strength against fully resisting opponents; (2) the combination and fitting together of similar core submissions, which also can be used at full strength and with maximum velocity; and (3) the use of off-balancing, or kuzushi, to expose opponents to the submission.

Together these three elements create the fundamental tactics that can be used in any situation in grappling. The submissions are always available; as long as they are in the same family or relation they can be used in combination; and off-balancing is used in the guard with sweeps as well as on the feet and throughout the scramble. It can be said that these elements are so strong that with them alone a guerrilla can have a long and productive career as a submission specialist.

A guerrilla understands that tactics always rule the battlefield, and he is prepared to do the work to understand all three of these elements. It is fine to have favored options, but for the guerrilla to be fruitful, he must master all three elements; to neglect any one aspect would be akin to entering the battlefield without bullets.

SECTION ONE: Core Submissions

Guerrilla jiu-jitsu's core submissions are the essentials of its finishing tactics. These movements are made up of Tier 1 techniques—those that can be practiced at 100 percent speed against 100 percent resistance and Tier 2 techniques—those that should be practiced with caution due to their inherent danger. Most Tier 1 attacks are traditional locks and chokes, while most Tier 2 submissions focus on ligament twisting, muscle slicing and compression, spinal and cervical cranks, and pain. Similar to firearm safety, guerrillas must train their submissions with due respect and must first seek knowledge of all core submissions.

For the guerrilla, most submissions will be built from Tier 1 attacks because of their ability to combine well with other Tier 1 or with Tier 2 submissions and because they can be practiced under the most realistic full-contact training scenarios.

SITREP 2.0 - THE VERSATILE JUJI-GATAME ARMBAR

SITREP 2.0 focuses on the juji gatame or cross-body armlock. Though often called the armbar in jiu-jitsu circles, Guerrillas see the juji gatame as an elbow lock. Full-body commitment to the hyperextension of the elbow joint makes this movement a devastating submission in any guerrilla's arsenal. As later discussed, the juji gatame can be used from nearly any position in grappling, including SITREP 2.0's closed guard version. This is a Tier 1 submission and game-defining finish for SUBJECT CAMARILLO.

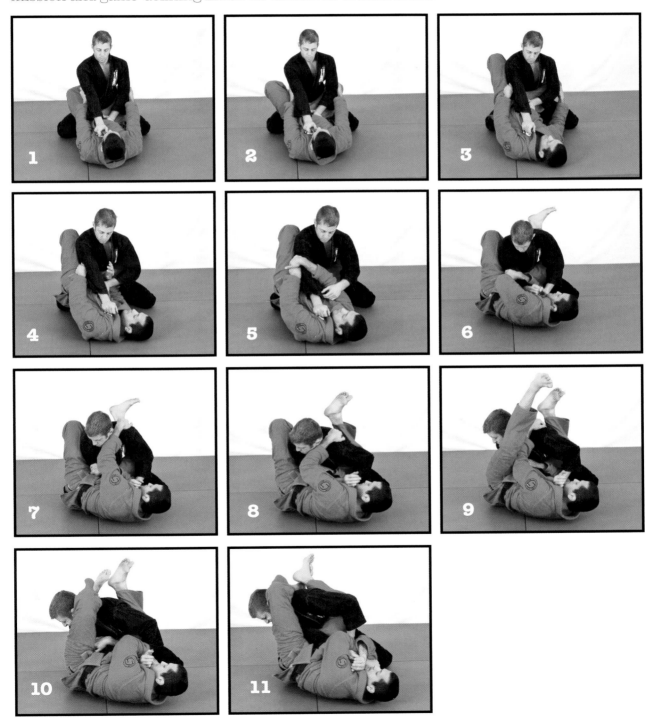

Plan of Attack:

a. SITREP 2.0 begins with SUBJECT CAMARILLO elevating his hips into the right armpit of CONTACT DARCY, MATTHEW. Camarillo exaggerates this movement to ensure control of Darcy's right arm while he continuously pulls on his right triceps grip control.

b. Camarillo furthers this control by wrapping his right arm over Darcy's arm to double the grip on his triceps. This creates a tight "back stop" control that prevents Darcy from pulling his endangered arm free. The trap is furthered as Camarillo escapes his hips leftward and pulls Darcy's arm to his center.

c. The guerrilla attacker moves to his attack angle by climbing his right leg high into Darcy's armpit for control. Combined with his foot pushing on Darcy's hip, this moves Camarillo to a perpendicular angle. He keeps his left arm braced in front of Darcy's head to prevent him from stacking or pressuring his weight forward.

d. With Darcy frozen in place from Camarillo's limb placement and hand grip, Camarillo easily has the time and space to loop his left leg over Darcy's head to lock the juji gatame. Camarillo hugs Darcy's arm and bridges his hips upward while creating downward pressure with his legs to hyperextend Darcy's right elbow.

SNAFU MOMENT:

If the guerrilla fails in the entry phase, he will remain in guard where he can safely renew the attack. If the opponent removes his arm after the angle has been made, the triangle should follow as a second line of attack. Stacking defenses will be analyzed in full detail later in the report.

When attacked from other positions, such as the mount, the same opportunities of retreat and attack are present.

AFTER-ACTION REPORT:

The juji gatame is a Tier 1 attack for guerrilla fighters that utilize a total-body commitment to hyperextend the opponent's elbow joint. Usually, an expertly applied submission at full force will result in tendon damage with possible outlying complications like dislocating of the elbow joint itself. Limb-breaking is exceedingly rare due to the hip action being away from the radius and ulna of the forearm, as well as the upper arm's humerus.

This movement combines well with all other Tier 1 submissions.

SITREP 2.1 - THE BLOOD CHOKE - SUBMIT OR SLEEP

Where arm and joint locks fail, blood chokes succeed. When faced with a resistant, powerful, or flexible opponent, sometimes locks are resisted. In the championship rounds, it is not uncommon to see a joint lock pushed past the breaking point with the victor leaving the mat with a displaced shoulder, snapped ankle, or ruined elbow. In these cases, the guerrilla must be prepared to blood choke for the win. SITREP 2.1 follows the blood choke, named for how it cuts off vital oxygen along arterial pathways, and its important place in the submission lexicon. Those that never submit to joint locks will go to sleep from choke holds. This is the power of this incredible tool.

Plan of Attack:

a. Attacking his opponent's vulnerable position, SUBJECT CAMARILLO brings his right arm across the neck of CONTACT DARCY, MATTHEW. By driving his hand to Darcy's collar bone, Camarillo ensures that both blades of his upper arm and forearm will be tight to Darcy's carotid arteries. To prevent Darcy's defense, Camarillo controls his left wrist.

b. Seeking more control, Camarillo brings his right knee to Darcy's right hip while he slides his left foot in front of Darcy's left hip. This allows Camarillo to fall into a controlling back position. Had Camarillo attempted this without the choking action, he likely would have failed as Darcy defended the back transition.

c. Camarillo falls to his back and places his right foot on Darcy's hip for pushing control while his left hook makes a belt line hook, readying him for a possible arm attack. With control established, Camarillo grips his right hand, hiding his left forearm behind Darcy. To finish, he squeezes both arms while hugging his head to Darcy's ear. This immediately cuts off blood flow to Darcy's brain and forces him to submit or pass out.

SNAFU MOMENT:

As with SITREP 1.2, a failed choke attempt should lead directly into an arm attack to continue pushing forward with the submission end game.

In the event that the choke is defended too early, attack the back control with hooks, when the opponent defends the hooks return to the neck attack. The opponent can only successfully defend one at a time.

AFTER-ACTION REPORT:

Though its image is brutal, the blood choke is actually quite painless. By focusing on the carotid arteries, the guerrilla expends far less energy than asphyxiation via windpipe strangulation. This movement is only effective when it cuts off blood supply to the brain, forcing limited bodily shutdown.

For the opponent, physical damage is only present when the choke is held long after the opponent has slipped into unconsciousness. Still, a guerrilla should train himself to feel when the opponent has passed out and respect him enough to release the submission immediately. It is also recommended that all guerrillas acquaint themselves with revival and resuscitation techniques such as basic, advanced, and infant forms of cardiopulmonary resuscitation (CPR).

It is recommended to attack chokes throughout training and competition, especially when faced with an opponent of stubborn mindset. If the opponent would rather win with a broken arm, make him go to sleep instead.

SITREP 2.2 - STRANGULATIONS - PAIN AND PRESSURE

There are few submissions that cause as much immediate fear, pain, and pressure as strangulations. For the guerrilla fighter, strangulations focus on a direct attack on the airway. Considered less efficient by some for their lessened effect on blood oxygen levels, these chokes are dangerous Tier 2 attacks on the trachea and its adjacent systems. SITREP 2.2 showcases the blade choke, which can possibly do major damage to the trachea with a slight choking effect on one carotid artery.

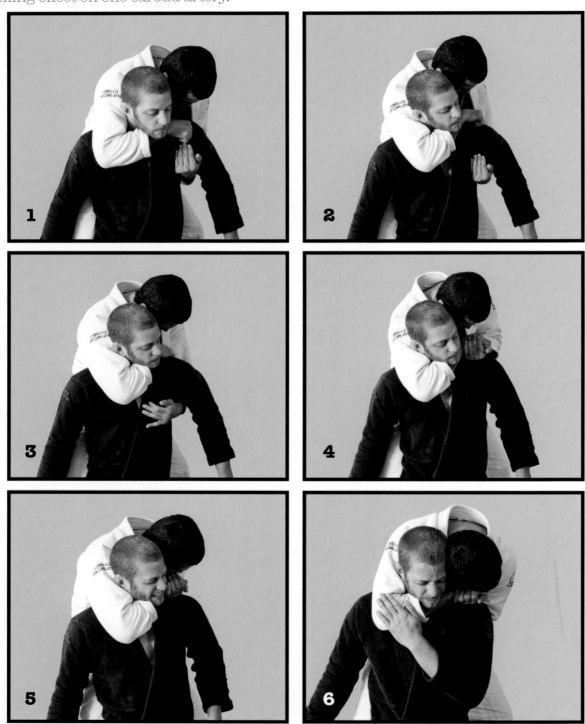

Plan of Attack:

a. In SITREP 2.2, SUBJECT CAMARILLO is attempting the rear choke on CONTACT DARCY, MATTHEW. Camarillo has attained a choking grip with his hand on Darcy's left shoulder and is about to remove his left hand from controlling Darcy's body to attack the finish. Darcy defends by turning his head to the left, relieving the pressure on his left-side carotid artery.

b. Sensing that the choke is lost, Camarillo continues to clasp his right hand with his left. He then hides his left forearm behind Darcy. Camarillo starts his squeezing pressure by pulling the blade of the radius bone of his right forearm upward and into Darcy's throat.

c. To finish, Camarillo drives his right ear to Darcy's left ear and pulls his right elbow tight to Darcy's collarbone. This sucks the forearm deep in an upward arc, compressing Darcy's trachea, causing an immediate submission from Darcy as the strangulation comes on with incredible force.

SNAFU MOMENT:

If the opponent manages to escape by pulling the guerrilla's arm and looking toward the elbow, the guerrilla can switch back to a rear choke. If he pulls the arm and faces the guerrilla's head, he may put himself in a particularly devastating choke: the Tier 2 rear naked neck crank.

Once the choke has reached the collar bone it is easily combinable with other cranks and strangulations.

AFTER-ACTION REPORT:

Where the blood choke looks brutal but is mostly painless and relatively safe, the strangulation is a windpipe compression that can cause damage to the trachea and area organs. In most cases, the choke only leaves a slight ache after first introduction. However, the compression does render it a Tier 2 submission that should be practiced with longevity in mind.

Practice this with precision and control, being sure to remove this pressure immediately after the submission has been signaled.

SITREP 2.3 - THE DEFLECTING OMOPLATA

The omoplata is a stealthy indirect attack that must be in the guerrilla's plan of attack. Though its angle of attack mirrors the ude garame bent armlocks, its approach is what sets it apart. By getting his body to the side, the guerrilla avoids nearly all stacking pressure while pursuing a top pressure of his own. This weight avoidance makes this an excellent tactic for smaller guerrillas that seek mobility in their attack strategies. SITREP 2.3 illustrates the difficulty in defending a strong omoplata assault.

Plan of Attack:

a. SITREP 2.3 starts with SUBJECT CAMARILLO escaping to a nearly facedown guard position with the left arm of CONTACT FERRISS, TIMOTHY, trapped under Camarillo's armpit. Whenever the arm is trapped here an omoplata is possible, and Camarillo has sprung into action. To get to the submission, he first pushes Ferriss's head away to make space for his leg to loop in front. Otherwise, Ferriss will be able to pressure Camarillo to his back.

b. Having created adequate space, Camarillo circles his right leg over Ferriss's head. As soon as his leg clears, he uses it to pressure into Ferriss. Next, Camarillo will seek to pull his legs out from under Ferriss to avoid his possible control or stalling tactics.

c. Camarillo is able to free his legs out from under Ferriss and has reached across Ferriss's lower back to prevent him from rolling forward in escape. Camarillo is careful to keep his leg heavy on Ferriss's left shoulder blade to prevent him from posturing upright in defense.

d. Using his left hand on the mat, Camarillo scoots his hips toward his posted hand while pulling on Ferriss's hip. This drags Ferriss's left hip to the floor and further prevents his ability to use posture as a defense.

e. Now that Ferriss is broken down to his left hip, Camarillo enters the end game. He turns his legs to his left side, allowing his upper body to lean rightward. Camarillo then finishes Ferriss by leaning toward his right shoulder, raising Ferriss's left elbow and effecting a strong twist on his trapped left shoulder. Ferriss is forced to submit.

SNAFU MOMENT:

Early in the movement, if the opponent tries to turn into the guerrilla, he will likely fall into a triangle choke.

If he counters later, two scenarios are often present: (1) If he rolls to escape before the hip is secured, the guerrilla can allow the roll and arrive on top or roll with him to finish the attack. (2) If he postures up, a back ukemi roll will also force the opponent to fall to his rear, landing the guerrilla on top. From here, he can roll again toward the legs to finish the omoplata.

AFTER-ACTION REPORT:

The omplata is a shoulder lock that places great force on the shoulder. It is a twisting submission by nature and is closer to Tier 2 status than the juji gatame armbar or choke. The goal of the guerrilla always should be to completely break down the opponent's posture and control his path of escape (POE) through proper hip control.

SITREP 2.4 - TRIPLE-SQUEEZE TRIANGLE

SITREP 2.4 analyzes the sankaku jime, or triangle choke, as it is better known. This versatile finish has become a hallmark of jiu-jitsu and submission wrestling as well as MMA's end game. It is as ingenious as it is effective. By dedicating the leg and core muscles against the relative weakness of an opponent's neck, the guerrilla is able to effectively blood choke while retaining great three-sided control of the adversary. Due to its ease in combining with the other submissions, the triangle is an essential Tier 1 combination drill.

Plan of Attack:

a. SUBJECT CAMARILLO is attacking CONTACT THOMSON, JOSH-UA, with a push-and-pull triangle setup. He has already driven Thomson's right arm inside of his legs with his left elbow grip while his right hand pulls Thomson's left triceps toward him. This automatically drives Thomson into this simple and efficient finishing technique.

b. If Camarillo keeps his hips low and heavy, he will likely fail as Thomson resists by posturing away. Instead, Camarillo uses his legs to bridge his pelvis close to Thomson's neck. Now, he is in range to break Thomson's posture and finish the attack.

c. With his hips and legs locked to Thomson's neck and head, Camarillo can now break his posture by pulling his hips back to the mat. As he drops his rear to the mat, Camarillo pulls Thomson's trapped left arm at the elbow to bring it across Thomson's own neck and body. Once trapped, Camarillo squeezes his knees and feet inward and downward for control.

d. Now Camarillo realizes that to finish with efficiency, he must change the angle of attack He grabs his left shin with his right arm and escapes his hips while preventing Thomson's posture. This pulls Camarillo's left leg across the back of Thomson's neck for the proper lock.

e. With his new proper angle, Camarillo reclasps his right leg over his left ankle and locks his palm-to-palm grip over both Thomson's head and his own left shin. To submit Thomson, Camarillo pulls down on this grip while pinching his knees together. Thomson is forced to tap as both carotid arteries are cut off.

SNAFU MOMENT:

If the opponent manages to escape into posture or free himself completely during the push-and-pull motion, it is usually due to the guerrilla pushing and pulling without popping his hips upward. A guerrilla has to know when to use explosiveness in his hips, especially in bridging actions such as this. Always make sure the push and pull coincides with the explosive hip bridge.

AFTER-ACTION REPORT:

As with all Tier 1 submissions, the triangle is best when your opponent's posture is under complete control. The guerrilla never forgets that this is a blood choke and not a neck crank. To ensure the blood choke, make sure the crossing arm is tight to the neck to cut off first the carotid artery. The second artery will be pressed with the inner thigh. The head pulling action is not to crank the neck — a strong opponent may resist the Tier 2 cranking action. Instead, pull the neck into the finishing arm and leg.

SITREP 2.5 - THE RAPID-ATTACK INVERTED JUJI-GATAME

For the guerrilla attacker, some submissions can work at a glacier's pace. Other submissions, like the inverted juji gatame, or straight armbar, work best when attacked aggressively. As a Tier 1 submission, this works well when combined with bent arm submissions such as ude garame kimuras, and Americana locks as well as the omoplata. Though setup is the key for all submissions, it is even more important for the inverted armbar. As made obvious by SITREP 2.5, the finish comes on very fast.

Plan of Attack:

a. By radically changing his angle through a facedown and hip escaping movement, SUBJECT CAMARILLO has managed to get to a great position to attack CONTACT FERRISS, TIMOTHY. Camarillo further establishes the attack angle by weaving his right leg under Ferriss's right armpit. This ensures that Camarillo will remain to Ferriss's desirable side position instead of the more difficult front-facing guard.

b. With Ferriss's left arm still trapped under Camarillo's armpit, Camarillo straightens his right leg while bringing his rear toward Ferriss. This puts a torquing pressure on both of Ferriss's shoulders, but it is not enough pressure to finish the submission.

c. Out of the pan and into the fryer. . . To break Ferriss's posture, Camarillo always aims for the head to keep him in the attack zone. Camarillo realizes the importance of fighting through to the attack zone and swings his left leg over Ferriss's head and adds downward pressure.

d. Even with the double shoulder pressure, Ferriss does not tap. Camarillo changes the attack by swimming his arm under Ferriss's left arm.

e. To finish with the straight armlock, Camarillo pins the arm to his shoulder and puts extreme downward pressure on the elbow joint with his right elbow. This drives Ferriss's elbow into the space between Camarillo's body and Ferriss's arm and hyperextends the elbow joint.

SNAFU MOMENT:

If the opponent forces his own elbow toward his hip to avoid the straight armlock action, the guerrilla can easily attack with the kimura. If the guerrilla does not have the same leg control as SITREP 2.5, he can also go to omoplata if the opponent defends. In the case that the opponent moves his arm to the forward position, the guerrilla can either do a forward roll armbar or swim his opponent's arm back into the straight-arm attack position.

AFTER-ACTION REPORT:

The inverted juji gatame, or straight armlock, should be done with speed and precision. Due to its speed, it is often used to frustrate the opponent's grip fighting as he tries to pass guard or defend mounted attacks. This makes the straight armlock an excellent technique to force the opponent to play more defensively out of fear of the quick submission finish. A guerrilla always makes his opponent fear everything.

SITREP 2.6 - THE COMBINABLE KIMURA

SITREP 2.6 focuses on the kimura lock of the ude garame submission family. As an ude garame bent arm attack, this submission forces the guerrilla to focus on the elbow and wrist to attack the opponent's rotator cuff and shoulder. This is a Tier 1 attack that can be attacked at speed when training, but it is close to Tier 2 status for the twisting action it places on the shoulder apparatus. Once controlled, this submission can and should be safe and it works well with other ude garame locks like the Americana, as well as triangles, armbars, and omoplatas.

Intro to Guerrilla Tactics

Plan of Attack:

a. SUBJECT CAMARILLO is ready to attack the right arm of CONTACT THOMSON, JOSHUA, as it is cleared to the floor and locked under his left armpit. Camarillo first needs to expose Thomson's elbow for the attack. He does this by bridging his hips into the elbow while pulling with his left grip on the triceps/elbow.

b. With the elbow open, Camarillo is able to cross his right arm over Thomson's shoulder and lock his right hand onto his left wrist to make a figure-four lock. Camarillo must make sure his right arm is above Thomson's elbow to keep the lock secured.

c. Camarillo falls onto his back; the pressure he applies to Thomson's right shoulder forces him to follow Camarillo to the mat with his posture broken. Now, Camarillo can add the finishing touches and finalize the submission.

d. To prevent Thomson's rolling escape, Camarillo crosses his left leg over Thomson's back and clamps down. This isolates Thomson in the downed position. Now, Camarillo looks to Thomson and elevates his left arm toward Thomson's upper back. This torques Thomson's shoulder and forces him to submit.

SNAFU MOMENT:

If the opponent drives forward to escape, he is actually assisting the guerrilla in his attack. The guerrilla never gives up on a control as strong as the kimura. Instead, the guerrilla shifts his hips to avoid the pressure and presses the lock.
If the opponent tries to explosively elevate backward to avoid the submission, the guerrilla follows him to either a hip heist reversal or transition into yet another submission like the guillotine or triangle choke.

AFTER-ACTION REPORT:

The figure-four lock of the kimura or ude garame family of submissions is one of the best controls in grappling. It is so dominant that it can almost be considered a position in and of itself. This move can be used from nearly every position and it is a great submission to link between positions and submissions. However, due to the twisting action, it should be regarded with caution for it nearly has Tier 2 status. Although this is a beginner technique, it can easily lead to torn rotator cuffs and shoulder damage when misapplied.

SECTION TWO: Basic Submission Chains

Where Section One covers the basic weapons profile of a guerrilla grappler, Section Two discusses how these work together to form the most basic of combinations and attack strategies. The objective for this section is simple: though the basic submissions themselves are often enough to effect a desirable finish, there will be times when a direct all-or-nothing attack will not be enough. As opponents improve and strategies get deeper, the guerrilla must understand how to put together his first attack chains.

These attack chains are guided by practical examples that give focus to budding guerrillas. Some attacks work better when combined with each other and this should be where guerrillas focus most of their attention while developing their first strategies for successful finishing.

The following section will delve into the relationship between armlocks and triangles and armlocks, kimuras, and straight arm submissions and beyond, as well as basic strategies to stay with the submission and see the fight through to the end. With this in mind, this list should not be seen as exhaustive, but instead as a way of approaching the art of grappling and a rubric for putting similar situations and submissions together to form a basic and overwhelming strategy for winning fights.

SITREP 2.7 - THE TRIANGLE AND ARMBAR RELATIONSHIP

The triangle and armbar are so intertwined that it is impossible to discuss the effectiveness of one without discussing the other. SITREP 2.7 showcases this relationship. If an armbar is forcibly or defensively lost, usually a triangle is available. Whenever a triangle is defended, an armbar opportunity presents itself. Perceiving posture and limb placement is critical, but even more important is feeling when to stick with attack or opting for another. SITREP 2.7 provides a great drill for going between the two related attacks.

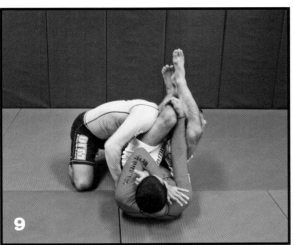

Plan of Attack:

a. SITREP 2.7 begins with SUBJECT CAMARILLO attacking the juji gatame armbar on the right arm of CONTACT THOMSON, JOSHUA. Thomson must defend by pressuring forward to close the space between his head and his elbow under duress.

b. Thomson explosively pulls his arm out of the armbar position and Camarillo immediately locks his legs around Thomson's head and left arm to trap the triangle position. Camarillo keeps his hips high to create a platform from which to slide Thomson's arm across to transition to the triangle position.

c. Having already cleared Thomson's right arm into a triangle attack position, Camarillo then grabs his left ankle with his right hand while his right leg posts on the opponent's hip or floor to escape his hips to a better attacking angle. This will make closing the triangle much easier and will give Camarillo a perpendicular position of attack.

d. As Camarillo transitions to close the triangle, Thomson ducks his head under Camarillo's left arm and starts posturing back and upward to escape the finish. Camarillo keeps his composure because he knows that the triangle and armbar together form a spiderweb of submission attacks.

e. As Thomson escapes the armbar by exploding upward, Camarillo follows by riding his momentum and crossing his right leg over Thomson's head. With his arm already crossed for the triangle, Thomson's elbow is very exposed and easily hyperextended by the sharp juji gatame armbar submission.

SNAFU MOMENT:

For the opponent to escape the final armbar he will have to return to a stacking position and is likely to try to turn the corner in a smashing type of pass. Once again, the answer is simple—return to the triangle and continue attacking this deadly one-two combination.

SITREP 2.8 covers other options off both the posturing and pressuring POA.

AFTER-ACTION REPORT:

This is an incredible combination that must be in every guerrilla's attack profile. The defense of one submission invariably leads to the other, but it will take fast reflexes to drive the opponent into the finishing lock or choke.

To build these reflexes it is important to drill the simplest combination of armbar and triangle and back again until the guerrilla can do this without effort or thought—make this a rapid reaction.

SITREP 2.8 - THE ARMBAR-TRIANGLE RELATIONSHIP

When developing combinations, the guerrilla has to understand how to (a)move into and between positions or submissions and (b)use the opponent's reaction to lead him to positions or submissions. SITREP 2.8 further analyzes the armbar and triangle by focusing on when to abandon one move for the other.

As a general rule, armbars are defended with forward or stacking pressure. Though this can ease elbow pressure, it also makes it much easier to lock a snug triangle. For the inverse, triangles are often defended with upright posture. This pulls the head out of the attack zone and eliminates pressure on the carotid arteries, but it also provides a moment to attack the re-exposed elbow joint with the juji gatame armbar.

A guerrilla understands these options and prepares to attack feverishly at the onset of either defensive posture or pressure.

Plan of Attack:

a. SITREP 2.8 opens with SUBJECT CAMARILLO attacking the juji gatame armbar against CONTACT THOMSON, JOSHUA. This is a mirrored finish to the example set in SITREP 2.7. However, this time Thomson actively defends by pressuring back into Camarillo to realign his hyperextended left elbow.

b. Thomson's downward pressure is welcomed by Camarillo. Instead of forcing the juji gatame, Camarillo begins circling his right leg out from in front of Thomson, while holding his own ankle to prevent the escape so he can lock the triangle hold. As he does so, he pressures with his abdomen to prevent Thomson from pulling his left arm out.

c. Camarillo locks the position by trapping his left ankle under the pit of his right knee. For the finish, Camarillo squeezes his knees inward while pulling down on his right ankle as he arches his left foot upward. If this is not enough, Camarillo grips his hands over his shin and pulls downward for an overwhelming choke.

SNAFU MOMENT:

The guerrilla must act swiftly when transitioning between triangles and armbars. If the guerrilla labors too long at point B. of SITREP 2.8, a strong opponent is likely to pull his elbow free. This will force the guerrilla into a defensive position where he must recover guard or transition quickly. Of course, the guerrilla should anticipate this inevitability and be prepared for his renewed attack.

AFTER-ACTION REPORT:

As long as the elbow is kept under control, the forward pressure of the opponent's defensive stack will always lead to a triangle submission. In a case where both arms are inside of the legs instead of one (as is the case in SITREP 2.8), the guerrilla must be patient and wait for the opponent to try to free his attacked arm. Once the arm is free, the guerrilla will attack the other arm, as it cannot easily escape the triangle lock. The guerrilla always uses his opponent's defense against him.

SITREP 2.9 - BLENDING BENT- AND STRAIGHT-ARM ATTACKS

The guerrilla understands that by straightening his arm or powering his arm into the straightened position, he is able to escape either the Americana or kimura (ude garame style) bent armlocks. So, instead of designing his strategy around forcing the arm back into the bent position, he is prepared to seize opportunity whenever his opponent straightens his arm in defense. In doing so, he creates an important medium between bent-arm attacks that allows him to continue attacking without unnecessary risk or movement.

Plan of Attack:

a. SUBJECT CAMARILLO is attacking the right arm of CONTACT THOMSON, JOSHUA, in a bent-arm kimura submission. Thomson must react quickly because his posture is broken and the lock of Camarillo's legs around his back is limiting his ability to roll free. Already, there is great pressure on Thomson's right shoulder.

b. To defend, Thomson forcefully straightens his right arm. Instead of forcing it back, Camarillo catches the arm on his near, or in this case left, shoulder. Camarillo traps the arm by pressing Thomson's wrist with his head, neck, and shoulder.

c. Immediately, Camarillo pursues the finish by turning onto his right side and bringing his left elbow clear over Thomson's right elbow, locking the position with a figure-four grip over his right forearm. Camarillo opens his legs, but pinches inward with his knees to control Thomson's mobility.

d. There is a gap between Thomson's right elbow and the mat, and that is exactly where Camarillo is driving Thomson's elbow. As he hyperextends the elbow, Camarillo is careful to squeeze his knees to prevent Thomson from climbing back into a closed guard position.

SNAFU MOMENT:

In a case where the guerrilla misses the near-side arm trap and the arm is cleared to the other side of the neck, the guerrilla can either (a) use a swimming (often called escrima or pummeling) type of movement to move the hand back to the near side or (b) follow the path of the arm and commit to a rolling juji gatame or forgo the arm attack and transition to the back.

AFTER-ACTION REPORT:

The straight armlock is an important go-between for bent-arm submissions. It provides a secondary submission between the kimura and Americana (often called keylock) submissions and it allows the guerrilla to fit three submissions that are easy to transition between into a similar window of opportunity. This creates a sensation of overwhelming offense, which is highly desirable for guerrillas.

Moreover, this attack series is also important because failure does not often result in the loss of position. As discussed in the SNAFU portion, there are plenty of secondary attacks such as kimura and omoplata as well as the reconciling of the closed guard attack hub.

SITREP 2.9 showcased a submission that naturally occurs off the defense of another. SI-TREP 2.10 evaluates a submission king that offers so much control that it can easily be used to pursue other finishes. In this situation, the kimura is analyzed for its ability to open up armbar submissions while protecting against the armbar's POE. Due to this nature, the kimura is a combination tool that should never be discarded. Even if the guerrilla does not feel strong with the kimura's finish, he must understand the way it is used to beat armbar defense.

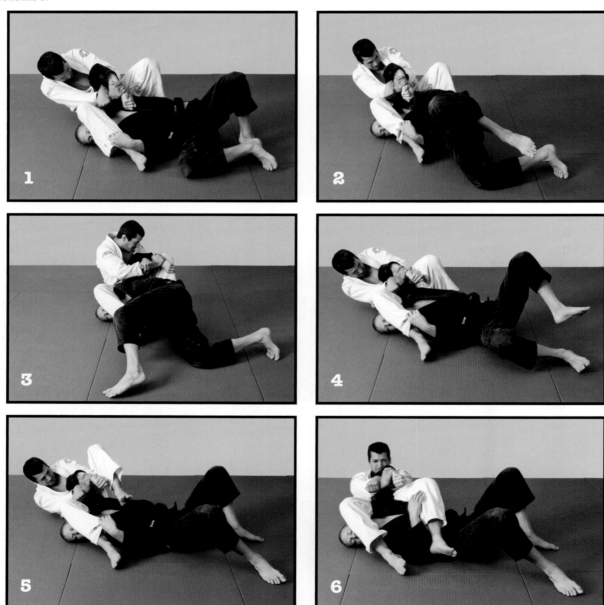

Plan of Attack:

a. SITREP 2.10 showcases SUBJECT CAMARILLO attacking what looks like a juji gatame armbar position with a kimura or figure-four lock on CONTACT DARCY, MATTHEW. This grip offers much more control for Camarillo than either a lapel, one-armed, or standard armbar grip. With this hold, Camarillo can control Darcy's entire body.

b. As Darcy attempts to roll away from Camarillo, Camarillo uses the kimura grip to torque Darcy's left shoulder. This immediately stifles Darcy's escape plan and blocks the POE with a submission roadblock. However, the angle is not perfect for Camarillo to finish the submission here.

c. With Darcy worried about the kimura pressure and the pain in his left shoulder, Camarillo can easily move back into the standard armbar position (SAP) and continue attacking the juji gatame armbar. Notice that he will not release the figure-four lock control, so he retains the ability to move Darcy at his own leisure.

SNAFU MOMENT—BE SURE TO TORQUE THE ARM:

The mistake here is to ignore the kimura torquing action and just try to step over from the SAP (standard armbar position) while holding the figure-four lock. This can result in the opponent rolling over his far shoulder and the guerrilla falling to his back with a much more difficult armlock to finish.

The guerrilla advice: use the kimura to dominate the top position and attack!

AFTER-ACTION REPORT:

The kimura is an excellent technique to combine with the juji gatame armbar because the elbow is already locked to the chest (if the guerrilla is attacking a proper kimura) and this is exactly where the armbar needs to be controlled. In addition, it provides an excellent control against rolling escapes and it provides torque and pressure that are often absent in armbar attacks by themselves.

The guerrilla understands this and knows that grouping similar submissions and techniques is fundamental to success.

SITREP 2.11 - THE KIMURA AS A FEINT TO ARMBAR

The kimura lock is such a strong submission that it often forces opponents out of their mindset and strategy as they desperately cling to absolutely anything to prevent the shoulder torque. With this in mind, the guerrilla always feints with the kimura to get this overly defensive reaction. From here, the kimura is more difficult, and the armbar is far easier. The guerrilla must understand how to drive the defense of the opponent to open up the easiest path to the submission.

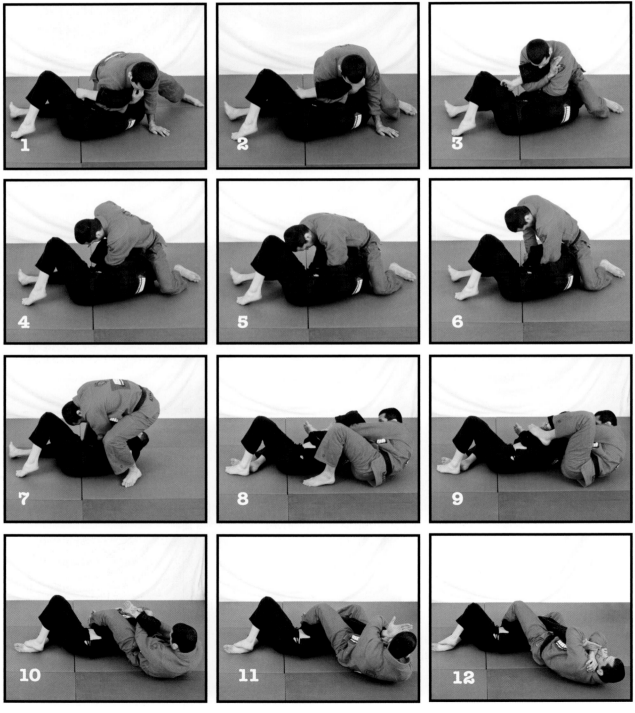

Plan of Attack:

a. SUBJECT CAMARILLO has the left arm of CONTACT DAR-CY, MATTTHEW trapped and is moving from a side control to a north-south control position. With his left arm under Darcy's armpit, he is in a position to remove his right arm to Darcy's left wrist and effect a figure-four control for the kimura submission. Already, Darcy is grasping toward his pants to prevent the possible submission.

b. With Darcy already preemptively locking down his arm, Camarillo easily obtains the figure-four for the kimura and jumps up to his feet, driving weight into the kimura grip. This weight on his chest keeps Darcy immobilized and allows Camarillo to change attacks as well.

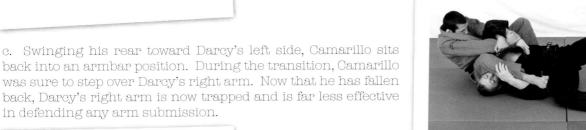

c. Swinging his rear toward Darcy's left side, Camarillo sits back into an armbar position. During the transition, Camarillo was sure to step over Darcy's right arm. Now that he has fallen back, Darcy's right arm is now trapped and is far less effective in defending any arm submission.

d. As with SITREP 2.10, Camarillo is able to use the kimura lock to prevent Darcy's shoulder roll. His right leg is trapping Darcy's right arm on the outside, which prevents him from using it to lever upward in escape.

e. Now Darcy can only defend with one arm, his arm that is under attack. Using his whole body, Camarillo easily takes advantage of this defensive hole and falls back into the juji gatame armbar to get the submission.

f. In the finishing position, Camarillo has his hips elevated to hyperextend Darcy's left elbow. His legs are heavy to prevent movement and his right leg is trapping Darcy's right arm to the outside to prevent its usefulness for escape. Camarillo has his entire body dedicated to controlling and hyperextending Darcy's left elbow.

SNAFU MOMENT:

If the opponent does nothing to defend the kimura when the guerrilla crosses into north-south, then he should finish the kimura submission. Although this is a feint, the guerrilla always has some intention to finish behind every single submission attempt. The best submission is the one that works! Do not overcomplicate by moving unnecessarily to a different attack.

AFTER-ACTION REPORT:

The kimura is used here to make a point to all guerrillas. It is often good to feed a defense to an opponent, especially if that defense makes other submissions or submission platforms easier to attain.

By attacking the kimura, the opponent feels it necessary to hold on to something to prevent the easy submission. That is the mark to move to the next submission platform, where it will be easier to control and overwhelm an opponent. In this case, the overly defensive mindset leads the opponent to be dominated.

SITREP 2.12 - "SCOUTING" SUBMISSIONS WITH SUBMISSIONS

Every submission has a multitude of other submissions to transition into and out of depending on the control and circumstance. However, to "see" these opportunities, the guerrilla needs to scout out submission controls to better understand when to move to a new attack or retreat to the original option. SITREP 2.12 focuses on playing with the kimura control to "see" the other options while the opponent struggles with the pressure and total body domination. Guerrillas should find these controls for all of their favorite submissions.

Plan of Attack:

a. SUBJECT CAMARILLO begins this drilling exercise with a tight kimura lock on the left arm of CONTACT DARCY, MATTHEW. Camarillo makes sure that his left forearm is keeping Darcy's left elbow trapped. If Darcy escapes the elbow, Camarillo can lose the position.

b. Immediately, Camarillo jumps to his feet and continues to drive the kimura lock into Darcy's own body. Camarillo uses both his right and left elbows as frames to create a boxed-in feeling for Darcy in combination with the chest pressure.

c. With Darcy under control, Camarillo can move from side to side and feel when the best opportunity is to move to Darcy's back, go to the kimura lock, or hunt other submissions like the armbar or positions like the knee-on-belly.

WHAT TO LOOK FOR:

Whenever the guerrilla goes "scouting," he needs to have incredible control over his partner. For this reason, the guerrilla uses the kimura in SITREP 2.12. With this control, he can look for armbars, bent armlocks, sankaku jime (judo triangle) chokes, the back position, north-south, the side control, and the knee-on-belly position while keeping the opponent completely under control.

AFTER-ACTION REPORT:

The guerrilla should go on scouting missions like this often, just so he is aware of how to positionally dominate his opponents while controlling their timing and postures. He should not only focus on the kimura as a scouting position, but also look to the armlock, triangle, and omoplata to learn how to seize control and transition to better submission vantage points.

SITREP 2.13 - THE CHOKE-ARM ATTACK RELATIONSHIP

SITREP 2.11 focused on using the defense of the kimura to set up arm attacks. The reason was simple, the kimura is so dominant it has to be defended and from that a new attack can present itself. The choke in SITREP 2.13 works the same way, but it uses the real threat of being choked out to create an even greater desperation. Obviously, choke defense must rely on the arms as a blocking device and these arms will be exposed to the attack as soon as the choking defense is prepared. Always attack with this in mind.

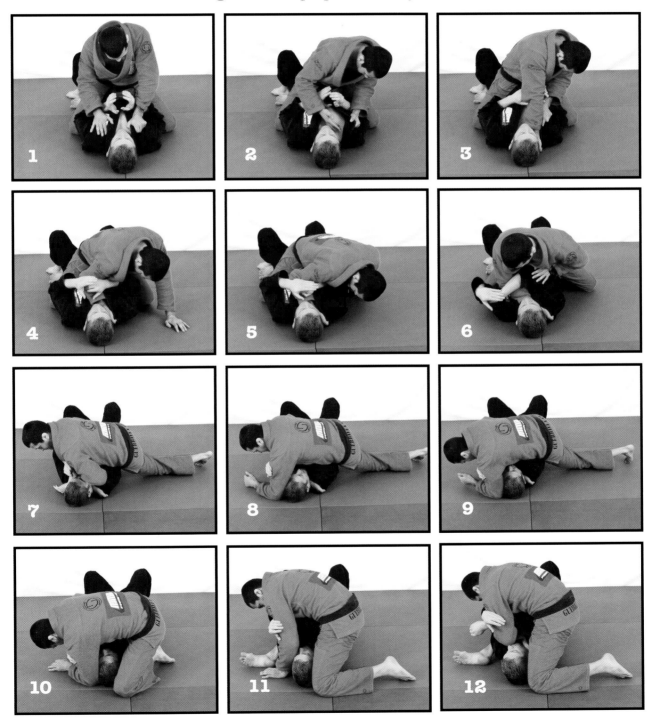

Plan of Attack:

a.   SUBJECT CAMARILLO begins mounted on CONTACT DARCY, MATTHEW. Camarillo does not waste time; instead, he immediately penetrates his left hand palm up into Darcy's right collar. Camarillo uses his left hand to slacken the collar and push on Darcy's arms to cause confusion. From here, Camarillo will drop his right elbow to block Darcy from weaving his right arm underneath in defense.

b. With Camarillo's right elbow pressing down on Darcy's chest, he has exposed Darcy's right arm. Darcy has no option but to use both arms to pull Camarillo's right arm away from its choking position against his carotid arteries. This serves to further expose Darcy's right arm.

c. Instead of simply pushing on Darcy's arm to trap it, Camarillo slides his whole body up to Darcy's right armpit so that his chest can trap Darcy's right arm against his face. Camarillo further consolidates the position by sliding his right foot under Darcy's left armpit for greater body control. Meanwhile Camarillo still creates choking pressure to keep the threat of the choke alive.

d. Camarillo weaves his left arm under Darcy's right arm to trap it and prepare for the leg-side armbar attack. Darcy feels the armbar coming and is crossing his left forearm over his wrist to preemptively defend the submission.

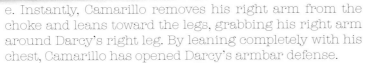

e. Instantly, Camarillo removes his right arm from the choke and leans toward the legs, grabbing his right arm around Darcy's right leg. By leaning completely with his chest, Camarillo has opened Darcy's armbar defense.

f. With Darcy's arm exposed from the leg-side turn, Camarillo can easily finish by falling toward the leg and committing to the leg-side armbar. He bridges his hips while squeezing his knees to hyperextend Darcy's right elbow.

SNAFU MOMENT—DEFEATING BODY TURNS:

As a general rule of thumb, in the case of SITREP 2.13, if the opponent turns to the right to escape (and pulls his elbow down to evade the arm attack), the guerrilla should return to the choke because the neck is open. If he rolls away (left) from the choke, the guerrilla can either immediately hit the fast transition armbar or take the back and finish with the lapel choke. Always attack what is exposed.

AFTER-ACTION REPORT:

By putting the opponent in a critical position (e.g. a choke), the guerrilla forces his opponent to either defend or submit. Think of grappling in simple terms not unlike the game of rock-paper-scissors. Being choked makes you sleep, arms defend the choke, and arms lose to armbars. So, keep this rock-paper-scissors scenario in mind and move between the submissions to force a good defensive opponent to submit from your relentless attack. Remember, the choke will always provide arm attacks, otherwise the guerrillas will leave a lot of their opponents asleep.

Staying with the submission is what creates a sense of dire urgency in your opponent. This is what creates fear and mistakes. Staying with the position is good for control, but if the opponent is excellent at surviving, he may not have as easy of a time with submitting. SITREP 2.14 focuses on using the submission as a transition between submission and position instead of solely looking at grappling as the transition between positions. This is essential for being a top finisher.

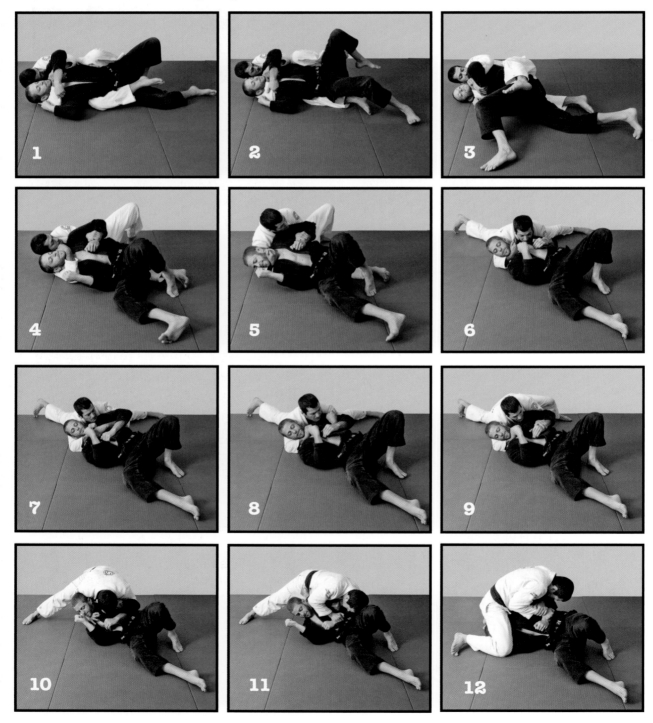

Plan of Attack:

a. The moment is captured with SUBJECT CAMARILLO on the back of CONTACT DARCY, MATTHEW. Darcy is defending the forearm choke and is sliding his right hip heavily over Camarillo's right leg to prevent the hook and escape to the mat. Camarillo counters by putting his left hook under Darcy's left thigh so that he can control Darcy's POE.

b. In one motion, Camarillo pushes off the mat with his right foot to create drive while he lifts with his left hook and left arm. This sends Darcy away from Camarillo and allows Camarillo to push himself to a top stable position.

c. Then Camarillo releases his right hand from the choking position, but continues controlling Darcy's head. While he does this, Camarillo must keep control of Darcy's left wrist and hand to prevent him from rolling away from the attack zone. This creates a kimura control on Darcy and limits his POE.

d. Next, Camarillo sprawls his weight to the mat, making sure that his chin and upper chest are over Darcy's left shoulder to prevent his mobility.

e. Instead of moving toward a stable north-south position, Camarillo wants the arm and is angling his body toward Darcy's left arm. Already, Camarillo is driving off the mat to force Darcy's left arm upright.

f. With Darcy's arm exposed, Camarillo can posture his hips up and drive his weight into the arm as if attacking the kimura lock control. This gives him the time to switch from a head control to the figure-four kimura grip.

g. Camarillo switches to a kimura grip, at which point he is not worried about the positional game of the back, side control, or knee-on-belly. His only concern is continuing to the finish.

h. Camarillo steps his right leg back over Darcy's head and has isolated the kimura for the classic finish. If Camarillo chooses, he can turn Darcy's arm to his front and then back to finish the bent armlock, or he can transition to yet another submission.

SNAFU MOMENT:

Guerrillas must not make the mistake of thinking that this is just one reckless submission after another. Do not just jump on the nearest thing that looks like a finish. Instead, steer your opponent using your hooks and grips and send him into another finish! The main point is still the same: to become comfortable between positions and use the submission to channel the fight in your direction.

AFTER-ACTION REPORT:

Though this situation is certainly an example of moving from a choke to a bent arm-lock, it is much more than that. This is a prime example of moving from a submission to a submission off of an opponent's escape. Instead of retreating to a better position, which is a good option, the guerrilla looks to finish the fight and is not worried about accruing points.

This is the heart of the guerrilla fighter and the guerrilla needs to learn to do this with his own personal fighting style, preferred techniques, and strategy. In this way, the submission becomes everything: the finish, the position, and the transition. When the guerrilla uses the submission as everything, he only gives himself the option for success with the finish!

SECTION THREE: Basic Off-Balancing & Submission Attacks

Though many guerrillas may scoff at the notion of using sweeps from the guard—after all, a sweep shows the inability to submit—they are wrong to forgo this important weapon in the guerrilla's weapons profile.

Sweeps work in many ways to create havoc for the opponent. They disrupt the opponent's balance and base, work well with submissions from similar grips and handles, and have the ability to either move the fight from the bottom to the top or force the opponent back into a more desirable attacking range. On the other hand, they are creative and often unexpected.

This unexpected nature makes them difficult to defend against, especially in the hands of a submission artist. If the opponent is always worried about submissions and the danger of every grip or hold, it will be easy to surprise him with a change of angle and an unbalancing reversal. Use this fear of the submission to make reversals easier.

However, before going further to analyze sweeps and their relation to the submission, guerrillas must understand that they are always submission fighters first. This creates a fear of the grip and a fear of the submission in their partners. This makes the sweep and the combination back to submission far easier. To make the sweep the focal point without submissions is a grave error. The opponent will learn to disregard the grips and eventually use base or balance out of the submission attempts, leading to failure and stagnation.

SITREP 2.15 - THE SWEEP TO THE IMMEDIATE SUBMISSION

The first example of bonding a sweep to the submission follows a successful sweep and its subsequent finish. It is best to use sweeping strategies that set the guerrilla up to finish when transitioning to the top. Often enough, one of two things happen: the guerrilla is able to drill through to the finish, or in the case of failure, the same finish is often still available from the guard position. Guerrillas must develop this skill of finishing with the submission not just the sweep!

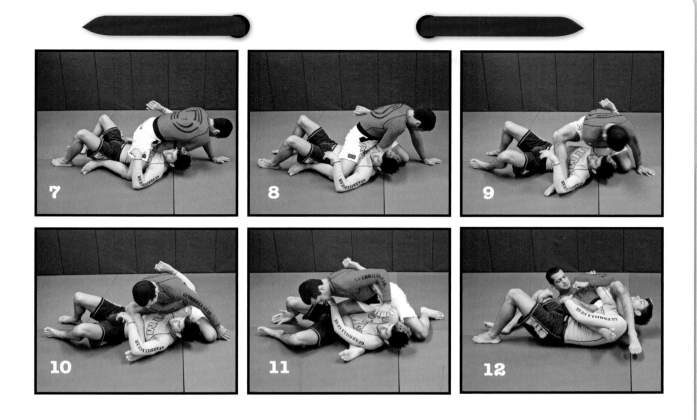

Plan of Attack:

a. SUBJECT CAMARILLO begins the sweep to submission from within his closed guard. Camarillo has broken down the posture of CONTACT THOMSON, JOSHUA, with both of Thomson's arms on the floor. To keep the distance close, Camarillo controls Thomson's neck and triceps.

b. As Camarillo feels Thomson trying to pull back into an upright posture, he releases his previous grips and allows him to sit up. Camarillo follows his momentum and reaches his right arm over Thomson's right shoulder, gripping behind his elbow. Camarillo makes sure to keep his hips driving forward into Thomson as his hand posts behind him to keep his balance (base).

c. Camarillo thrusts his hips forward and topples Thomson back over his legs and hips. Without delay, Camarillo rides the momentum into a high mount, trapping Thomson's right arm under his armpit. To ensure that the arm remains in position as Camarillo transitions to a better attack position, he pulls Thomson's elbow with his right hand, pinning Thomson's right arm into his armpit.

d. Now it is time for the armbar. Camarillo lifts his right leg and begins moving to the perpendicular position.

e. To get his left leg over Thomson's head, Camarillo collapses his base toward his right side, moving into a classic S-mount position. This takes the weight off his left leg and allows it to easily cross over Thomson's head. Meanwhile, Camarillo hugs Thomson's right leg before falling back into the armbar position.

f. With all the pieces in place, Camarillo quickly crosses his leg over Thomson's head and falls backward into the leg-side armbar position. He pulls on Thomson's leg while pushing down with his own legs as he lifts his hips and pinches his knees to hyperextend Thomson's right elbow.

SNAFU MOMENT—LACK OF RESOLVE:

The biggest SNAFU is to focus too much on the sweep and congratulate yourself too much for making the points. This tends to lead to a segmented game where every move is done independently. In doing so, the fighter puts the brakes on every movement after its individual success. This is worrying too much about points. Instead, learn to sweep and continue the momentum through to the finish. This will lead to more submissions because the best time to finish is when the opponent hasn't had the time to recover or think. Catch him off guard and take the kinks out of the sweep-to-submission transition.

AFTER-ACTION REPORT:

When the opponent wants nothing more than to avoid submissions, the sweep has to come into play, whether to reverse the situation or open the opponent to future submissions. In this scenario, it is vital that the guerrilla plays forward and aggressively moves clear through to the submission.

Though there are many ways to use sweeps in a submission-focused game, always remember that the threat to reverse the situation is real!

SITREP 2.16 - THE ATTACK ZONE AND FAILED SWEEPS

SITREP 2.16 teaches to use the sweep to control posture. If the opponent's posture can be brought back into control, then the opponent can be driven into the attack zone, the area where the guerrilla has the most attacks at this disposal and the opponent has very little. This area is found when the opponent's posture is completely broken down or he is transitioning from the broken posture to an upright posture. Learn to break the opponent down to this area using sweep attempts and resume the attack.

Plan of Attack:

a. Similarly to SITREP 2.15, SUBJECT CAMARILLO is hip heisting forward and into CONTACT THOMSON, JOSHUA, while reaching over the shoulder in a classic hip bump sweeping maneuver. In this case, however, Thomson is driving against Camarillo and fighting to push the guerrilla fighter to his back again.

b. Thomson successfully avoids the sweep by driving against Camarillo's sweeping action and forcing his back to the floor. However, Thomson's posture is completely broken and now he is in danger of submission attacks such as the kimura lock. Camarillo understands this and prepares to attack off the posture change.

c. As Thomson postures up, Camarillo pulls Thomson's elbow, pushes off his hip with his left foot, and climbs his right leg high into Thomson's left armpit. His left hand braces against Thomson's face to prepare for the armbar.

d. All that is left is for Camarillo to cross his left leg over Thomson's face, raise his hips while pressing down and inward with his legs, and secure the wrist. This combined action hyperextends and controls Thomson's right elbow and forces him to submit.

SNAFU MOMENT—THE OPPONENT STALLS:

The guerrilla understands that at any moment the game can change or the opponent can decide to do something out of the norm. In the case that the guerrilla is forced back to the mat and the opponent decides to stay there and stall, there are two strong options: (1) Attack the kimura/guillotine combination or (2) bait him into reposturing and then attack again!

AFTER-ACTION REPORT:

SITREP 2.16 is dedicated to using the sweep as a control device. For this and any similar situations, it is crucial that the guerrilla finds his attack zone and the preferred attacks from within it. In this particular example, it was the fight to regain posture that the guerrilla took advantage of. Other possibilities for guerrilla attacks can come from standard posture-breaking techniques and reposturing, although the guerrilla often prefers sweeps because there is the chance of offensive reversal and top game transitioning.

SITREP 2.17 - USING SWEEP FEINTS TO SET UP SUBMISSIONS

All feints in guerrilla jiu-jitsu have an element of reality behind them. Nowhere is this truer than in the example provided in SITREP 2.17. The guerrilla must acquaint himself with using sweeps to sweep, but he also must have his plan B prepared in case the opponent defends and can be led into a submission. In contrast to SITREP 2.16, the goal here is not to get to a platform to attack (the attack zone or an attacking platform) but to use the opponent's reaction to directly feed into the finishing lock or choke.

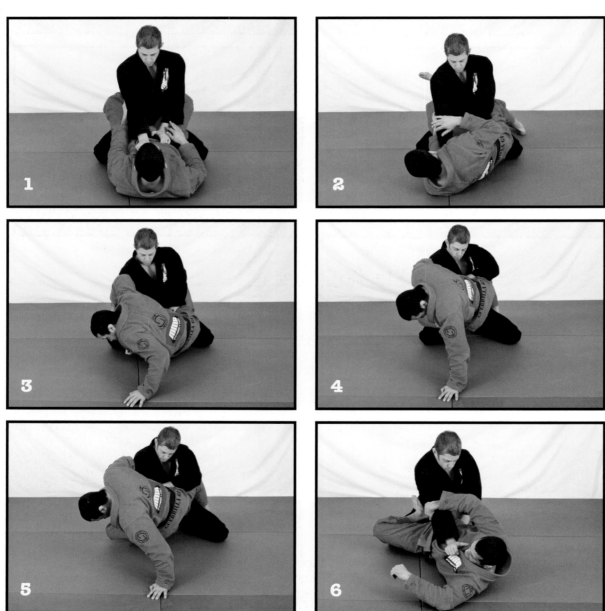

Plan of Attack:

a. SITREP 2.17 opens with Camarillo controlling the right triceps of CONTACT DARCY, MATTHEW. Darcy is fighting from an upright posture and Camarillo is already shifting onto his left side for his POA (plan of attack).

b. In one explosive maneuver, Camarillo thrusts his hips forward into Darcy's midsection and replaces his left triceps grip with his right arm over Darcy's shoulder. The angle of the attack is lower than in SITREPs 2.16 and 2.17 as if he is trying to roll Darcy to the side. Notice that Camarillo posts with his left hand on the mat for balance and the ability to push with his hips.

c. With immense pressure pushing him to his right side, Darcy braces with his left arm, opens up his knees to establish a greater area of base and uses incredible abdominal strength to push back into Camarillo. This is what Camarillo is waiting for, and he puts his left foot on Darcy's hip while they are momentarily frozen in struggle.

d. In a radical change of direction, Camarillo falls to his back in a perpendicular arm attack angle. He uses his foot on Darcy's hip in a classic armbar setup as he uses the momentum of the direction change to clear Darcy's arm across his body.

e. Without delay, Camarillo secures Darcy's wrist with his left arm and circles his left leg over Darcy's head. Darcy has pushed Camarillo to the mat and fallen directly into his waiting spiderweb.

f. Camarillo drives his leg over Darcy's head and explodes his hips upward. Darcy's right elbow is hyperextended and he is forced to submit.

THE IMPORTANCE OF RIDING THE MOMENTUM:

This movement should be executed with lightning speed from the onset of resistance. The guerrilla must work tirelessly to develop the sensitivity to know when to change the angle and pounce on the kill. If he takes too long to identify it, the moment may be lost, especially when facing a great opponent. Learn to identify the moment through training and work on a smooth transition through to the finish.

AFTER-ACTION REPORT:

SITREP 2.17 successfully illustrates the need to use feints to get to the game ending submission. In this case, the feint feeds directly to the armbar, but if the opponent does not react to the feint, the guerrilla must be prepared to finish the sweep and transition to the top submission.

It is advised to play with lower and higher angles on sweeps, even if they put the sweep at an awkward angle, for the benefit of creating easy transitions to the finish.

SITREP 2.18 - SWEEPING FOR A BETTER ATTACK ANGLE

The guerrilla must understand how his opponent regains his base off of sweep attempts and use this knowledge to set-up subsequent attacks. In this regard, the guerrilla once again frustrates his opponent's defenses and leaves him exposed for the submission. This is different than finishing the attack - this is a mindset of breaking an opponent down to get to the submission. Use near sweeps to get more and more submissions off the scramble - this is a great opportunity for the fast win!

Plan of Attack:

a. SUBJECT CAMARILLO begins with control over the triceps and sleeve of CONTACT DARCY, MATTHEW. Darcy is using a staggered grip and upright posture to debilitate Camarillo's submission game.

b. Lifting his hips slightly, Camarillo swings his right arm under his body until his hand can grip the outside of Darcy's right knee. While he is reaching, Camarillo also moves his centerline toward Darcy's right knee as he moves forward in his POA (plan of attack).

c. With his weight moving over Darcy's right side, Camarillo now puts his left foot on Darcy's hip and rocks him off balance with his left leg. Due to Camarillo's extreme right-side posture, Darcy feels light on his left side and is easily unbalanced.

d. In one motion, Camarillo pulls on Darcy's right knee while rocking down with his right knee. This topples Darcy to the mat in a near sweep position.

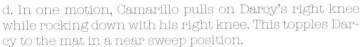

e. Instead of releasing the grips and fighting for a top position that he may or may not get, Camarillo secures the arm, shifts his hips under Darcy's elbow and bridges his hips upward to finish the very fast armbar.

FEELING OUT NEAR SWEEPS:

It is critical that guerrillas attain a feel for near sweeps, because they are great opportunities to finish the fight. No one wants to be swept, especially in a situation where the sweep can lead to a mount. A guerrilla must understand this and know how to control the near sweep just long enough to transition to the submission. A game made of near sweeps and submissions is very hard to beat.

AFTER-ACTION REPORT:

By understanding the opponent's need for base and survival, the guerrilla can devise a game plan that takes advantage of the scramble and finishes the fight before the need for guard recovery or forced sweep.

Every guerrilla should look to his favorite sweeps and work on how the opponent will scramble to safety. There is a submission in that moment—work on the control for that near sweep, and finish.

CONFIDENTIAL INFORMATION

1209-83-68-888

Assembling a Fire Base

FILE 003: ASSEMBLING A FIRE BASE

Every guerrilla must have at least one fire base to call home. An expert guerrilla will have many. For budding guerrillas, the fire base or HUB is both a place of refuge and security as well as a strong platform for launching attacks. It can be a position or in some situations a submission, just as long as the guerrilla has clearly defined approaches and strategies to reach it.

This ease of access is essential for all HUB fire bases. If the road is inaccessible and the base is blocked off, then there better be another option to bypass the roadblock or the guerrilla may be in trouble. In this regard, the guerrilla grappler must define several alternate routes to his favored attack base. Beyond this, it is vital that he also looks to Murphy's Law so that every tangible counter and obstacle is accounted for when creating his paths to the fire base.

Defensively speaking, the guerrilla should also be ready to fall back to the fire base. If the fire base is within the closed guard position, such as the Octopus HUB, it would be much preferable to get rolled into the Octopus HUB than to simply be reversed into the closed guard where the guerrilla still must work to get to his desired attacking position. As a position itself, the fire base must be defensible against all classic and unorthodox positional escapes.

When it comes to offense, these are the best positions for a guerrilla to launch attacks from. The guerrilla's highest percentage submissions should originate from these positions; therefore, these are the positions that guerrillas should seek out most expeditiously. Once within these areas, the guerrilla should seek an 80 percent or higher submission success rate.

When personalizing one's own fire base, it is great to start with the favorite top position and bottom position and then define the types of submissions most preferred to find from that fire base. For instance, if the spider guard is the favorite position and triangles are preferred, the guerrilla should seek out a HUB that includes at least one foot on the biceps and a proper hip lift and angle to execute triangles as well as at least two other secondary attacks. With this example, the guerrilla would not rest in spider guard but push through to the spider HUB where attacks come consistently with higher success.

OCTOPUS HUB

Every guerrilla should have at least one fire base on the bottom or guard position and one on top. For SUBJECT CAMARILLO, the preferred bottom fire base is the Octopus HUB. Using the Octopus HUB, Camarillo can enter submissions and reversals as well as take the back while constantly deflecting the forward pressure of the opponent. Following is an exposition on Camarillo's enters, controls, and attacks from this focal point for the guard.

ENTERING INTO A BOTTOM FIRE BASE: OCTOPUS HUB ENTRY

For the stand-up fighter, wrestler, or judoka, the entry is everything in a fight. Without it there is no need for a vast repertoire of submissions and attacks. With entries, everything becomes available. For the bottom guerrilla it is critical to develop some variety in how to enter into the fire base of choice. As with all aspects of grappling and guerrilla life, preparation and execution are key.

SITREP 3.0 - ESTABLISHING A BOTTOM FIRE BASE

Most HUB positions rely on entries from neutral or slightly favorable positions and the Octopus HUB is no different. SITREP 3.0 originates from a closed guard position where the bottom guerrilla has an opportunity to finish the fight or reverse the position, but the top player can use weight and positioning to stifle attacks and possibly survive or pass the guard. Therefore, the guerrilla opts to change the angle of attack and advance to the Octopus HUB, a position where he can deflect the opponent's weight and lead him to defeat.

Plan of Attack:

a. SUBJECT CAMARILLO is using the closed guard position against CONTACT FERRISS, TIMOTHY. Ferriss has attained a strong upright posture with forward staggered hands to prevent Camarillo from sitting upright or from being pulled downward. Camarillo realizes that he must move to an attack HUB where he has more options for attack. He grabs Ferriss's right wrist and pushes against his right knee to setup the transition.

b. Camarillo counters Ferriss's posture by shifting his body onto his left hip and stiff-arming his right arm away from Ferriss. As he does so, he sits up onto his left hand to further close the distance with Ferriss. This expertly diffuses the power of Ferriss's formerly posted left arm.

c. Unsatisfied to remain to Ferriss's front where he can possibly be pressured back into closed guard, Camarillo uses his right foot on Ferriss's hip to escape his hips to the outside and he places his left foot on Ferriss's hip for an attack position. From the Octopus Guard, Camarillo is one move away from taking the back, armlocking, or submitting his opponent.

SNAFU MOMENT-DEALING WITH PRESSURE:

The SNAFU moment comes when the guerrilla does not continue in the face of pressure. Be steadfast and determined to sit up and do not flop back to the mat at the first sign of resistance. This is why learning to move continuously and with purpose must be emphasized early for all budding guerrillas.

AFTER-ACTION REPORT:

The strength of the Octopus HUB comes from avoidance and deflection. By moving out to the side and thrusting the opponent's pushing hand away, the guerrilla is better able to control his opponent than from a traditional closed guard. The opponent loses the ability to effectively distribute his weight forward, whereas in the traditional closed guard he can effect a certain level of pressure by leaning forward.

As with other HUB positions, the Octopus forces the opponent to react by resisting forward. This will lead to the following fast submissions.

ATTACKING FROM A BOTTOM FIRE BASE

The fire base from the bottom must be dedicated to greater control than any ordinary guard position. It also must be a place where attacks can be launched and, if necessary, a place to retreat when in danger. The following are some examples from SUBJECT CAMARILLO's preferred bottom attack base—the Octopus HUB.

SITREP 3.1 - BOTTOM SUBMISSIONS WITH THE OCTOPUS HUB

The measure of any great fire base or HUB is in its ability to set up strong submission attacks that play off the opponent's reactions. Fighting from the Octopus HUB easily accomplishes this as most reactions feed into myriad Tier 1 and 2 submissions. Whether it is SITREP 2.3's omoplata, SITREP 2.5's inverted armbar, or the following triangle submission, this position is ideal for using gravity as well as the opponent's defense/discomfort to feed many high-percentage finishes.

Plan of Attack:

a. SUBJECT CAMARILLO moves his right hand to the neck of CONTACT FERRISS, TIMOTHY, after previously using it to hold Ferriss's right wrist open long enough to feed his right foot under Ferriss's right arm. Camarillo also pulls his left foot to Ferriss's hip so it is ready to either attack, push Ferriss away, or open up Camarillo's hips to propel him farther toward Ferriss's back. This completely eliminates Ferriss's base and will eventually force Ferriss face-first into the mat.

b. Without any hands to either stop his descent or block Camarillo's attacking arms, Ferriss is in trouble. Camarillo understands this and uses his free right hand to assist in pulling his left leg in front of Ferriss's right shoulder. Ferriss feels the triangle coming, but with his arms entangled, there is little he can do at this point.

c. Camarillo falls to the mat and uses his left hand to pull his knee into the right side of Ferriss's neck, creating discomfort and a choking action. It is important that the guerrilla creates discomfort in the submission from start to finish and not just at the end point.

d. With Ferriss's posture broken forward, Camarillo can release the hook under his right arm and lock the triangle position. Camarillo continues his knee-pinching squeeze throughout the movement. For many, this will be enough to finish the fight.

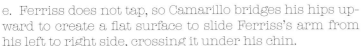

e. Ferriss does not tap, so Camarillo bridges his hips upward to create a flat surface to slide Ferriss's arm from his left to right side, crossing it under his chin.

f. With Ferriss's arm crossed, Camarillo returns his hips downward, locks a Gable grip over his left shin for downward pressure and finishes with a strong downward pull and inward pinch of the knees. Ferriss is forced to tap to the highly efficient choke.

SNAFU MOMENT:

If the guerrilla loses the under-the-armpit trap and the opponent tries to push forward, there are plenty of viable submissions such as the omoplata or the face-down armbar (rolling juji gatame). As always, a great option is to return to the Octopus HUB by retrieving the wrist, but if this is not possible, the remaining trapped arm should be attacked expeditiously.

AFTER-ACTION REPORT:

Whether it is with a triangle, omoplata (SITREP 2.3), inverted armbar (SITREP 2.5), or another submission, the Octopus HUB proves itself to be a strong attacking position. By trapping both arms and adjusting both the attackable and defendable angles, this becomes a much stronger attack platform than the closed guard on its own. By using gravity and the lack of posture in your opponent, this HUB becomes absolutely devastating in the right hands. This is the strength of using HUBs from the bottom position; it makes the bottom overwhelming and it turns the tide of any match.

SITREP 3.2 - WHEN TO USE REVERSAL WITH BOTTOM HUBS

The best time to execute a reversal is at the moment of resistance to a submission or sweep. However, when is the time right to leave a strong bottom fire base with so many familiar submissions? In this case, the time is right because (a) the guerrilla understands that he will land in a strong S-mount HUB position with multiple submission opportunities and (b) the opponent on top is focused solely on hiding from the submissions and forcing the submission will be more difficult than moving to the strong S-mount on top.

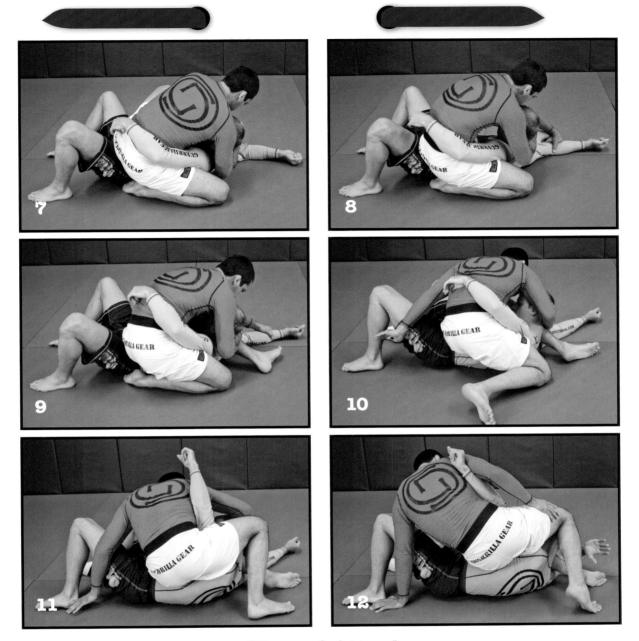

Plan of Attack:

a. SUBJECT CAMARILLO is in the Octopus HUB with CONTACT FERRISS, TIMOTHY. Ferriss has been submitted before and is using all of his strength to prevent Camarillo from hooking his right foot under his right arm. Camarillo begins his counter by pushing his hips further onto Ferriss's back as he looks downward to the mat.

b. Using the same action as the hip heist sweep, Camarillo drives his hips into Ferriss while his right arm pulls Ferriss's basing right arm off the mat and his left hand pushes his weight into and on top of Ferriss. This forces Ferriss to fall to the mat in a mounted position with his left arm trapped.

c. Camarillo does not release the right arm. Instead, he slides his right knee deeper into Ferriss's armpit and leans slightly to the left to lighten his own left foot. Camarillo prevents the leftward roll by driving Ferriss's right hand onto the mat.

d. To make matters worse for Ferriss, Camarillo exchanges grips on the right arm so that his right arm can wrap around Ferriss's head into a shoulder trap. This puts Tier 2 cranking pressure on Ferriss's neck and diverts focus away from his trapped arm and onto the neck, a secondary target at this point.

e. With his left leg lightened from the S-mount position, Camarillo easily slides it over Ferriss's right arm and behind his neck. Camarillo continues to trap Ferriss's right shoulder and pull his head off the mat to inhibit Ferriss from bridging or escaping. Meanwhile, Camarillo brings his left hand to the front of Ferriss's left hip to further restrict movement.

f. Balancing on his left hand, Camarillo brings his right thigh upward, keeping his shin close to Ferriss's neck. Then, he finishes the trap by clasping his right thigh and bridging his hips upward. With Ferriss's arm trapped under Camarillo's armpit there is no chance of escape and he is forced to signal the submission.

SNAFU MOMENT - DEALING WITH THE ROLL:

Depending on timing, getting rolled should not be too large of a problem. If rolled before the leg is crossed over the opponent's arm in the S-mount, then the guerrilla should return to his preferred bottom fire base (in this case Octopus HUB) and not just the guard.

If rolled after the leg is crossed over the arm, the guerrilla should execute a strong pulling action to ensure that the opponent follows him into the triangle submission. With this in mind, do not fall into the triangle, but pull into the finish!

AFTER-ACTION REPORT:

As with all bottom fire base positions, the Octopus HUB must have an avenue to sweep the opponent when he defends every submission attempt. In actuality, he also should have an avenue for escape as well (i.e. standing up out of the guard).

In this regard, the Octopus HUB has the same fighting parameters of the closed guard, but due to the proximity and attack angle, it is better suited to a larger variation of immediate and easy-to-accomplish submissions and reversals.

It is recommended that all guerrillas seek out their own bottom fire bases, whether they are from open or closed guard in origin or based off of semi-completed submissions (e.g. the loose or dirty triangle as a HUB).

STANDARD ARMBAR POSITION HUB

    The Standard Armbar Position or SAP is SUBJECT CAMARILLO's preferred top fire base. As with any strong top HUB, the SAP consists of great control, many submission possibilities, and transitional opportunities to other top controls.

    The SAP consists of two main controls: Leg-side when the guerrilla controls the arm with his head-side arm and head-side when the guerrilla controls the arm with his leg-side arm.

LEG-SIDE

HEAD-SIDE

ENTERING INTO TOP FIRE BASE: SAP ENTRIES

Entries into the top fire bases are usually incredibly varied. Due to the nature of being a specialized top control, these can often be reached through sweeps, failed submissions, guard passes, and positional transitions. For SUBJECT CAMARILLO, that goal is to reach the SAP from anywhere that he can quickly transition to one of his many primary grip breaks and arm submissions.

SITREP 3.3 - MOVING BETWEEN FIREBASES/SAP ENTRY

A methodical guerrilla knows that fire bases offer familiarity as well as defensive and offensive capabilities. Therefore, in order to get to his personal higher-percentage attacks, he should utilize movement between HUBs to get to submissions. In SITREP 3.3, the guerrilla expertly slides from an already superior position, the mount, to a more dominant attack fire base, the S-Mount. From here, he continues to the Standard Armbar Position (SAP) where he can execute any number of joint locks or submissions.

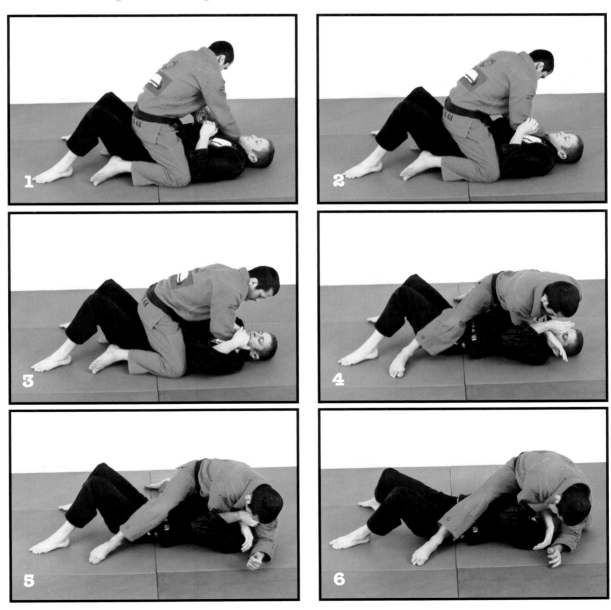

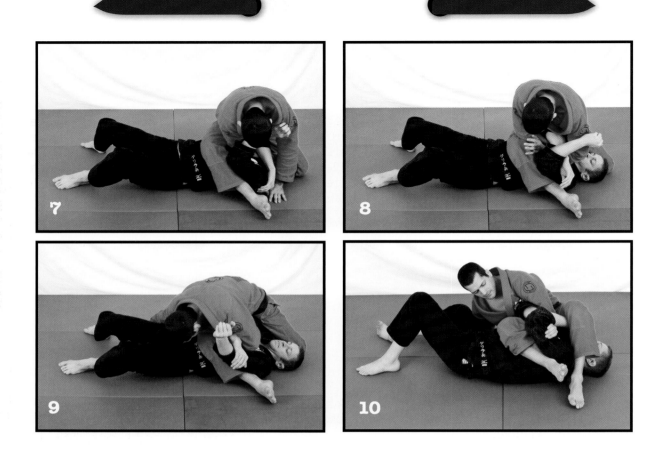

Plan of Attack:

a. SUBJECT CAMARILLO begins SITREP 3.3 from the mounted position over CONTACT DARCY, MATTHEW. Camarillo has a lower upright mount with both hips over Darcy's hips. His right hand is in a cross-lapel choking grip and his left hand is posted on the floor for stabilization.

b.   As Camarillo drives his chest over Darcy's right arm, he slides his left knee deep into Darcy's armpit. By elevating the mount, Camarillo will be able to attack chokes and armbars in unison while maintaining immense pressure over Darcy's chest. Darcy realizes this and crosses his arm to prevent the possible juji gatame armbar.

c. Camarillo drops his left elbow to the floor in front of Darcy's left ear and moves Darcy's head to the right. This opens up his neck for the choke and forces Darcy to close in his hands and elbows to block off space for the choke and armbar.

d. With Darcy's arms close to his body, Camarillo can easily slide his right foot toward Darcy's head to seal the S-mount. From the S-mount HUB, Camarillo can choke, wrist lock, take the back, and attack the arm.

e. Because Camarillo is most comfortable with juji gatame arm-locks he moves to one of his favorite fire bases, the SAP HUB. He does so by crossing his left leg over Darcy's head and blocking his right hip with his right hand in a leg-side SAP.

WHEN TO GO FOR THE SUBMISSION:

Through the transition from the mount to the S-mount to the SAP, there are ample opportunities to finish the fight and they should all be considered. From the second the cross-lapel grip is made, the guerrilla must believe he can submit his opponent. If the opponent's defense opens up, the finish should happen here. Likewise, if the armbar presents itself from S-mount (the opponent stays on his back or rolls too far too one side), the guerrilla should attack from there. It is always about the defense. With this in mind, a guerrilla is ready to finish but is capable of taking a great opponent to the easiest-to-finish fire base as possible. In this case, it is the SAP position where he can attack with the most confidence.

AFTER-ACTION REPORT:

By transitioning between fire bases, the guerrilla develops a positional game between the major positions of mount, back, side control, and knee-on-belly. Instead, he develops the control and grappling IQ to see where he needs to be to best execute a submission-focused game.

If one was miles from home and lost without water, would he rather take the path where he has the most access to streams or just try to get lucky running through the foliage?

SITREP 3.4 - MOVING FROM THE BOTTOM TO TOP (SAP) HUB

Just as the guerrilla is forced to transition from a top position to a bottom fire base, he also must learn to move from the bottom to his high-percentage HUB on top. In SITREP 3.4, the guerrilla sweeps to the SAP HUB when his opponent defends his juji gatame armbar. Regardless of this transition or others, the point is the same—you should always have it in your mind to find your HUB position.

Plan of Attack:

a. SUBJECT CAMARILLO begins in the open guard position with CONTACT DARCY, MATTHEW kneeling in front of him with one knee dropped on the mat. Camarillo has taken a sleeve and lapel grip and his right foot is on Darcy's inside knee.

b. Camarillo pulls his rear to his heels to close distance with Darcy. As he does so, he places an outside hook (De la Riva hook) with his left foot inside of Darcy's right hamstring and his right foot moves to Darcy's hip. As he drives forward and lies back, Camarillo also pulls Darcy toward him to off-balance him forward.

c. With Darcy's balance broken forward, Camarillo can easily lift his hips off the floor by extending his legs upward in a leg press motion. As he does so, he releases his De la Riva hook and steers Darcy's upper body in a counterclockwise motion with his grips to set up the angle for the armbar.

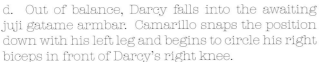

d. Out of balance, Darcy falls into the awaiting juji gatame armbar. Camarillo snaps the position down with his left leg and begins to circle his right biceps in front of Darcy's right knee.

e. By pushing down with his legs and pulling with his arm, Camarillo is able to reverse Darcy into the SAP position. From here, Camarillo has the positioning and patience to attack continuously toward the finish.

AFTER-ACTION REPORT:

The guerrilla must understand his own strengths and weaknesses. If he does not have a strong HUB position from the bottom, he must use favored sweeps and reversals to get to his top HUB. This is good for the attacker. Not only does it outline these strengths and weaknesses, but it also provides a definable mission for the bottom guerrilla.

The next step in personalizing this is to define the guerrilla's highest-percentage sweeps and reversals that are easiest to execute, and then to link these to the top HUB. In the clean-up phase, the guerrilla will troubleshoot this game plan and further develop it through academy training.

This third entry into the SAP position (behind SITREPs 3.3 and 3.4) focuses on two converging elements: surprising the opponent with a nontraditional approach to a typical problem (in this case passing the guard with a kimura roll) and using the unorthodox to blaze a path to the desirable fire base. In SITREP 3.8, the guerrilla uses both elements as he kimura rolls over the seated guard to arrive in not just the kimura lock, but the SAP HUB as well. Surprise, creativity, and élan are all essential elements to a guerrilla grappler.

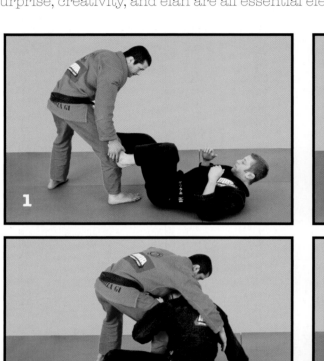

Plan of Attack:

a. SITREP 3.5 opens with CONTACT DARCY, MATTHEW sitting forward in a seated guard/single-leg position with SUBJECT CAMARILLO, DAVID.

b. As Darcy sits forward, Camarillo realizes that Darcy must use his right arm for base and is ready to take advantage of that. He reaches his right arm over Darcy's right shoulder and grabs under his armpit. Camarillo makes sure to keep Darcy's head tucked inside his right flank to keep his back from being exposed.

c. Camarillo locks the figure-four lock on Darcy's right arm and then commits to a forward roll over his right shoulder. As a focus for the roll, Camarillo will project his feet hard to the mat to ensure that Darcy arrives on his own back.

d. Once he lands, Camarillo escapes his hips toward his left while he punches the kimura grip into Darcy. By punching the grip, Camarillo inhibits Darcy's movement and prevents him from easily sitting up toward him.

e. With the kimura lock in place and his hips escaped, Camarillo immediately goes for the armbar. Darcy counters by pulling his arm inward with all his might.

f. Instead of battling the arm, Camarillo adjusts the position by sitting forward into the SAP. In this case, Darcy has released his arm and will be finished immediately. If he had stayed with his defense, he would have gone through either leg-side or head-side SAP attack positions.

SNAFU MOMENT—The opponent escapes his head during the roll:

If the opponent escapes his head during the initial roll, the guerrilla's back is exposed. He must alter the roll by using his hips to push into his opponent's head and then throw his hips beyond his opponent's forehead. He does not want to roll forward in this case because he will risk exposing his back.

AFTER-ACTION REPORT:

Unorthodox attacks, creativity, and a go-for-it spirit assist guerrillas time and time again. In this case, the guerrilla does not attempt to pass and fight for inches when he can see the finish line in sight with the exposed rear arm.

Whenever there is a high chance for submission, especially if it is through a high-percentage platform like a fire base, the guerrilla should always know his directive—to attack.

SAP LEG-SIDE TO HEAD-SIDE SWITCH

When switching from a leg-side to head-side SAP position and back, it is best to take a finger-clasping grip and pull the arm through. This is much faster than feeding a new hand through one at a time, and speed is often key to successful attacks! The guerrilla must also replace the rear posting hand to avoid being rocked/bridged into a bottom armbar position.

SITREP 3.6 - DIRECT FIRE BASE FINISHES - LEG SIDE SAP

The easiest, and more often than not fastest way to submit from a fire base is to go the direct route. The best time to attack direct finishes from HUBs is to immediately attack from the transition into the fire base. Time is essential! The longer a guerrilla takes for direct action, the more likely the chance of the opponent clamping down his defense with more power. In SITREP 3.6 the guerrilla immediately transitions into the standard leg-side armbar from the SAP.

a. SUBJECT CAMARILLO has landed in the leg-side SAP with CONTACT DARCY, MAT-THEW, on the bottom. Camarillo controls Darcy's arm with his left hand, making sure he is securing Darcy's forearm while his right hand holds Darcy's right leg.

b. Keeping his left hand clamped on his own lapel, Camarillo begins falling toward Darcy's legs for the submission. He holds Darcy's right leg throughout the maneuver.

c. Camarillo levers Darcy's arm free by pulling at the forearm and wrist with all of his body weight and using a negative angle (like a kimura) to drive the arm free.

d. Keeping Darcy's leg to ensure he doesn't move to his knees, Camarillo squares his hips, adds upward hip pressure, and hyperextends Darcy's right elbow.

When direct action maneuvers fail, the guerrilla always has contingency plans. Remember, for any HUB or fire base position, the guerrilla must intimately know nearly every contingency for every attack, counter, and transition conceivable. After all, this should be the guerrilla's go-to position to which all other positions are channeled. In SITREP 3.7, the direct action of 3.6 has failed due to aggressive or strong resistance and the guerrilla must change gears to an equally aggressive direction for the submission.

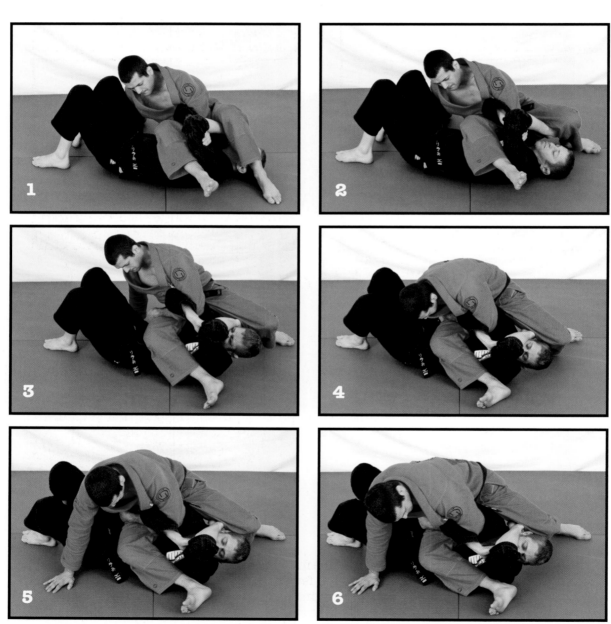

Plan of Attack:

a. SUBJECT CAMARILLO has already attempted the leg-side armbar of SITREP 3.6, but the defense of CONTACT DARCY, MATTHEW, was too strong. Instead of continuing with the direct leg-side attack, he has removed his leg from over Darcy's head and has sat forward into a near SAP position.

b. In the same motion, Camarillo keeps his forward momentum as he sits up farther across Darcy. Though Camarillo maintains his original grips, his left leg now presses back slightly behind him to provide a pushing forward pressure while his head crosses over Darcy's body toward his left hip.

c. With Camarillo's forward pressure, his body weight now presses Darcy's right elbow, making it incredibly difficult for Darcy to escape by shucking his elbow downward. Camarillo places his right hand on the mat in front of Darcy's left hip to inhibit movement and provide stability for the coming submission.

d. While Darcy keeps his left arm "waiting" for Camarillo's left leg to cross over the head, Camarillo acts. He uses his left hand to punch Darcy's left elbow upward, exposing his right arm for the armbar.

e. Without delay, Camarillo slides his left shin in front of Darcy's neck and face, bases with his right hand on the floor, and boosts his pelvis into Darcy's right armpit. To finish, Camarillo thrusts his hips forward and arches his back to hyperextend the elbow joint and force the submission.

SNAFU MOMENT-SECURING THE ARM:

With SITREP 3.7 and 3.8, along with all arm attacks from SAP and elsewhere, securing the arm is incredibly important. Speed does not mean to attack haphazardly and lose the armbar 5 out of 10 times. Only work as quickly as possible without losing the armbar due to a weak grip or setup. Always armlock the forearm and wrist and not the elbow, and secure the arm with total-body dedication.

AFTER-ACTION REPORT:

Even when a direct armbar fails, a good guerrilla sticks with the attack and focuses on a couple of concepts: overall tightness and wrist angle. For tightness, is the pelvis driving into the armpit? Are the knees pinching the arm securely? Are the legs distributing body weight effectively? For wrist angle, is the wrist vertical with the thumb in the upright position? If so, there is little to worry about an elbow being shucked out or the opponent rolling to freedom. In this situation, the guerrilla does what he knows—he continues the attack.

SITREP 3.8 - FIRE BASE SAP - FULL-BODY ASSAULT

Often enough, a fighter will get tunnel vision and focus solely on one element or body part when trying to obtain the finish from the SAP. This can be a great error. In SITREP 3.8, the leg-side SAP break serves as an excellent example of using the full body to break the grip and finish the attack. While keeping a strong pulling action on the arm, the guerrilla is able to creatively use a free leg to pry the elbow free and expose the arm. This is possible due to good positioning, weight distribution, and full-body commitment.

Plan of Attack:

a. SUBJECT CAMARILLO is in the leg-side SAP, with his left arm securing the arm of CONTACT DARCY, MATTHEW while his right hand controls his near-side leg and hips. Darcy has taken preventative posture by clamping down on his exposed right arm with his entire left arm.

b. As Camarillo attempts to cross his leg over Darcy's face, Darcy keeps his arm in front of his face to block Camarillo's leg from coming over. If Camarillo drops his leg over Darcy's upper forearm, he may be rocked backward from an escape attempt or pressing maneuver from Darcy.

c. Camarillo realizes two things: he must incorporate more of his body into the attack and he must avoid Darcy's roadblock. He deftly continues his circling movement, bringing his left shin and hooked foot under Darcy's left elbow. Immediately, Camarillo uses his leg to start forcing Darcy's defensive grip upward.

d. As Camarillo forces the grip upward with his legs, he weakens Darcy's grip and spreads the defense over too wide of an area. With his defense outstretched, Camarillo can now incorporate his standard leg-side armbar action to expose the arm for attack.

e. With Darcy's right arm exposed, Camarillo can fall toward his leg into the juji gatame armbar. Camarillo finishes with hips high and a classic rear naked grip over the wrist, showcasing total domination of the position.

SNAFU MOMENT - DEALING WITH THE SIT-UP:

With the guerrilla's leg crossing under the arm instead of over the head, some opponent's will try to sit up in defense. This is an inevitability and it is easy to prepare for. For the leg-side armbar, as in SITREP 3.8, it is key to control the near-side leg or possibly take a weaving grip to control both, and to stretch the body long during the attack. This will prevent the opponent from sitting up and initiating an escape into the guard.

AFTER-ACTION REPORT:

By having faith in the leg-side SAP positioning and grip-fighting tension, the guerrilla learns to feel when and where he can use free limbs or body parts to better effect the grip breaking. The point however, is to dedicate the entire body to the attack. One part is pulling to create tension, one part is pushing to lock the opponent to the mat, and the free leg is there to pry the arm free.

SITREP 3.9 - FIRE BASE SAP - TWISTING FINISH

SITREP 3.9 displays the ingenuity of a finish that only comes when a guerrilla learns a few important lessons: control, patience, and body mechanics. When these come together, the fighter will have the time and positioning to effect devastating grip breaks and finishes like this. For the example, the twisting finish is not only creative; it is practical. Through the twisting motion, the guerrilla forces the protected arm into a bent armlock like the Americana. This creates a prying effect that is nearly impossible to resist.

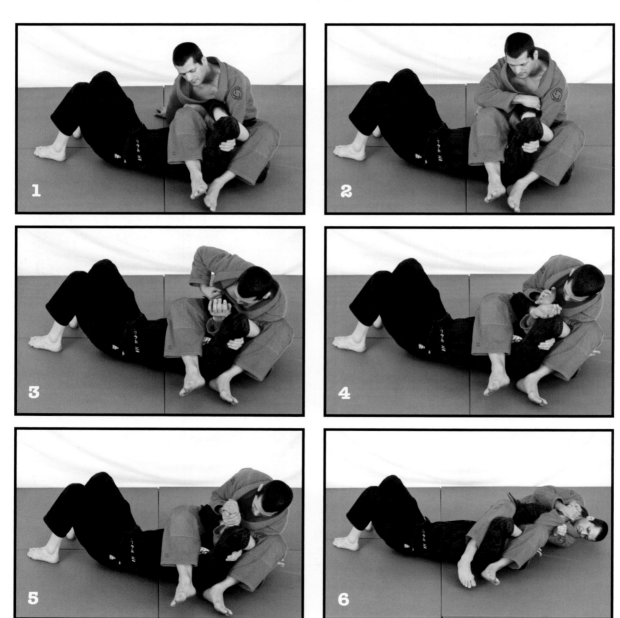

Plan of Attack:

a. SUBJECT CAMARILLO is in the leg-side SAP with CONTACT DARCY, MATTHEW defending by intertwining his left arm over his right in defense and hiding his left arm inside. This creates space for Darcy and helps in the clamping effect of saving his arm.

b. To break the hold, Camarillo first hides his right elbow inside of Darcy's right arm on the head side. As soon as the elbow is tucked in deep, Camarillo clasps his hands in a palm-to-palm grip.

c. Using his right arm as a wedge, Camarillo pulls with his left arm and upper body against Darcy's right wrist. This creates a torquing motion similar to the Americana bent-armlock.

d. Camarillo senses that the torquing pressure is having the desired crow-bar effect and drives his body toward the head side to pop Darcy's arm free. Immediately, Camarillo secures his wrist and hand to prevent Darcy from escaping over his left shoulder with a roll away.

e. To finish, Camarillo rolls back to his hips-square position, rear naked grips Darcy's wrist, hammers down with his legs, and bridges his hips upward to hyperextend Darcy's right elbow.

SNAFU MOMENT—THE DANGER OF A HEAD-SIDE ROLL-OUT:

The danger of a head-side rollout is real anytime the guerrilla falls toward the head to finish. However, there are plenty of counters as long as the wrist is kept under control. For one, the wrist can be torqued back to force the return to the armbar, or the position can be changed as the guerrilla falls into either the omoplata or triangle attack. The key is total arm control and that starts at the wrist.

AFTER-ACTION REPORT:

The twisting grip break and finish is not just a simple breaking technique—it is an Americana bent armlock. The guerrilla must realize this to have success with this type of an attack. In fact, the bent arm lock motions (Americana and kimura) are not only great submissions, but incredible controls and grip breaks as well. Learn to use all your submissions to assist you, whether it be to open up other submissions or to finish.

SITREP 3.10 - FIRE BASE SAP - X BREAK

The head-side X break is another full-body grip break that expertly introduces range into the equation of grip fighting. For SITREP 3.10 the use of both legs is not simply cosmetic. By stretching both crossed hooks inside of the assisting (defensive) arm, the guerrilla is able to push the opponent's defensive clasp to its limit. The guerrilla understands that certain grips like the clasp can easily be pushed to the limit as long as he can create the range to keep both arms stretched.

Plan of Attack:

a. SUBJECT CAMARILLO has attained the head-side SAP and is looking for the armbar against CONTACY DARCY, MATTHEW. Camarillo has fed his right foot inside of Darcy's defenses in the hops of breaking his grip. At this point, Camarillo has Darcy's defense severely outstretched and has forced him to hold a hand-clasping defense with all his might.

b. Camarillo slides his left leg under his right to help with the grip break. To divert Darcy's attention and to prevent him from defending the maneuver, Camarillo pulls with his grip and extends his leg to keep Darcy clinging to his defense instead of focusing on Camarillo's left foot.

c. Without stopping, Camarillo continues to slide his left foot all the way through, until he can lock his toes against Darcy's left triceps. He curls both feet together as if to hold Darcy's arm. Meanwhile, Camarillo rear-naked grips the right arm.

d. To break the grip, Camarillo explosively extends his hooked feet forward while pulling back with his mid- and upper back. The pressure is too much against Darcy's clasped grip as his hands break free from one another.

e. With the defense released, Camarillo puts weight on his legs and falls back into the juji gatame position. Camarillo will keep a strong hooking pressure throughout the submission to keep Darcy from escaping.

SNAFU MOMENT—MISSING THE SECOND HOOK:

Whenever a guerrilla grips with both legs as hooks, there is a precarious moment where the guerrilla's balance may be out of sorts. In the case that the guerrilla falls to his back with only the leg-side leg slid through, he should immediately control the head and attack either a triangle choke or triangle armbar. To avoid falling to the back, the guerrilla must focus on distributing weight between his grips and the one leg to avoid being bridged backward.

AFTER-ACTION REPORT:

At the heart of the X break is knowledge that the hands-clasped grip is weak. This grip does not effectively engage larger parts of the body to defend smaller ones. Instead, it takes a relatively weak element, a grip, and defends it with another. By stretching the arms to the limit, these grips are taxed. Once they are at their breaking points, it only takes the weight of the body falling backward to slice through this defense like a hot knife through butter.

Guerrillas always need to have the ability to control their space, and a part of this, as shown in previous examples, is the removal of obstacles to open opportunities. SITREP 3.11 focuses on the removal of the supporting arm. For the attacker, this arm is a real nuisance; it can lift weight off the head and deflect attacks while keeping its primary responsibility, the defensive arm, secure. In this case, exposure and removal of that arm becomes paramount to a successful triangle armbar submission.

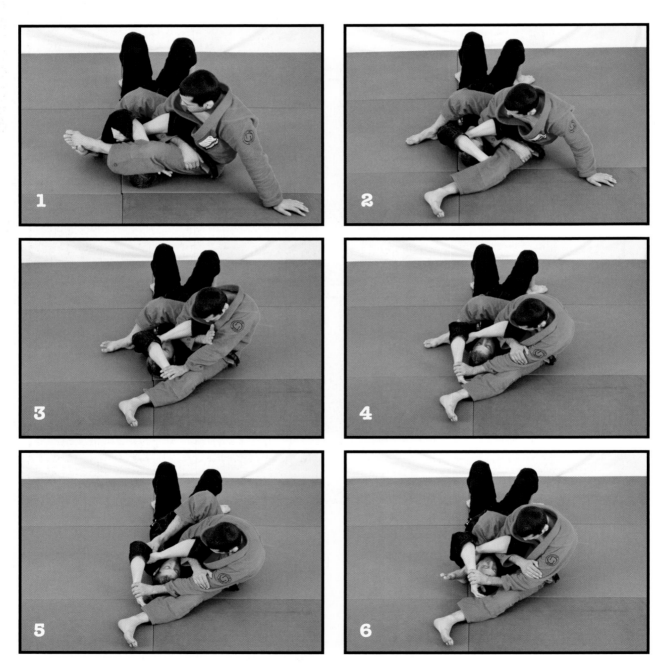

Plan of Attack:

a. SUBJECT CAMARILLO is in the head-side SAP and has attempted to cross his leg over the head of CONTACT DARCY, MATTHEW, to initiate the grip-breaking series. Darcy has been here before and has defended the technique by securing his left biceps and hiding his left arm under Camarillo's leg. Instead of letting Darcy push his leg off his face, Camarillo counters by removing the leg himself to expose the pushing hand.

b. With Darcy's left hand exposed, Camarillo is able to secure it at the wrist with his own free hand. Camarillo pushes it away until it is no longer a factor in Darcy's defensive gameplan.

c. Next, Camarillo slides his right leg inside of Darcy's left biceps on the head side. Camarillo does not release any of his previous grips. Darcy feels that the pressure has released from his body as Camarillo's upward pointing knee has created a pocket of air for him.

d. Darcy seizes the opportunity, but walks into a trap. He rolls into Camarillo thinking he can escape the armlock. Camarillo reads this perfectly and switches to a figure-four lock as Darcy rolls into him.

e. Darcy begins to feel the trap being sprung so he shifts his weight to the right as he tries to free his right shoulder and arm. Camarillo drops his right foot to the mat to prevent this escape and he drives his knee downward to pin Darcy's shoulder to the mat.

f. With Darcy momentarily immobilized, Camarillo quickly locks the triangle position by locking his right shin under the pit of his left knee. Camarillo points his left toe downward for added pressure.

g. To finish the hold, Camarillo sits up to his left hand and faces downward. As he does, he pulls the grip to his chest while bridging his hips laterally. The motion is fast and severe, forcing Darcy to submit from a hyperextended right elbow.

SNAFU MOMENT—A LACK OF AGGRESSION:

Unfortunately, many budding guerrillas lose this position as their opponents manage to shuck their arms out of the triangle before it is locked. This leaves a guerrilla on his back with his legs in a double underhooks passing position. This is not good for the guerrilla, but it is a situation he will have to deal with while learning to tighten the position and attack aggressively to stay on the advantage.

AFTER-ACTION REPORT:

If the supporting arm has become too much trouble for the guerrilla attacker, he must get rid of the problem. Grappling is often like mathematics in that there is an order of operations. If the arm can possibly be used to defend the armbar or escape, should the guerrilla just insist on his current unsuccessful operation? Of course not. Take care of the immediate problem first by overtly getting rid of the problem—the supporting arm—then the attacks should come much easier.

SITREP 3.12 - FIREBASE SAP - ARMBAR SWITCH

Out of failure comes success to those that are prepared. SITREP 3.12 expertly captures this sentiment with its armbar switch. In this situation, the inability to use SITREP 3.11 to eliminate the supporting arm leads to an opportunity to switch armbars. The guerrilla must prepare for the inevitability that his opponent will push his head-side leg off his face to escape and again, he should prepare to counter with a submission like the armbar switch.

Plan of Attack:

a. Similarly to SITREP 3.11, SUBJECT CAMARILLO is in a head-side SAP attacking the left arm of CONTACT DARCY, MATTHEW. Again, Darcy has a good defense, and this time he has managed to push Camarillo's leg off his face while he uses his legs to bridge. This is a good strategy for Darcy, as it has forced Camarillo's weight forward and created an opportunity for him to escape to his side.

b. Darcy has seized the moment and the space he has created by further pushing Camarillo's leg away and shucking his right elbow toward the mat. At this point, Camarillo feels like he is losing the left elbow and will have to change gears.

c. Camarillo's first counter is to use his left hand on the mat to push his hips forward and into Darcy to prevent him from reaching his knees.

d. Then, Camarillo releases Darcy's right arm and switches to a control on his exposed left arm. Camarillo's body prevents Darcy from shucking his arm free, so Darcy continues his momentum and fights to get to his knees.

e. As Darcy reaches his knees, Camarillo crosses his right leg over to the armbar position on Darcy's left arm. Camarillo squeezes his knees together to control the arm and prevent the escape.

f. Without delay, Camarillo pushes his body off the mat and drives his hips downward into Darcy's left elbow. This forces Darcy to submit in the downed position from a hyperextended left elbow.

SNAFU MOMENT—THE LIMP ARM ESCAPE:

If the opponent manages to "limp arm" out of the facedown armbar, indicating a failure in grip strength and control on the guerrilla's part, the guerrilla should turn the corner and go to the opponent's back to begin attacking anew. This is available because the guerrilla has maintained his posting arm and is in position to easily transition around the corner.

AFTER-ACTION REPORT:

The guerrilla clearly understands that the opponent must stiff-arm the head-side leg very hard to press a leg off his face. After all, a leg is usually pretty strong and moderately heavy, especially a leg that is trying to control an armlock! By resisting a little, the guerrilla can guarantee a strong push and it is this momentum and exaggeration that the guerrilla feeds on to switch to the other arm for the attack. In this way, the opponent may think he is escaping, but he is really only slipping deeper into the web.

SITREP 3.13 - FIREBASE SAP - DEFLECTING POWER

Some opponents may seem just too strong or powerful when trying to break the SAP stalemate. In these cases, the interrelation of weight distribution and baiting will come in handy. The guerrilla always understands how to place his weight to make his opponent uncomfortable. In doing so, the pressure will become the bait, as the stronger opponent will usually resist with a push and it is this push that will be capitalized on with the revitalized attack.

Plan of Attack:

a. SUBJECT CAMARILLO is in a leg-side SAP, controlling the right arm of CONTACT SWICK, MICHAEL. Swick is defending by securing his left biceps to keep his right arm bent.

b. Camarillo realizes that Swick may be too large and strong for his standard attacks and removes his left leg to drive his body weight over Swick.

c. As Camarillo pushes off the mat with his left foot, he moves over Swick to his left side. Camarillo keeps balanced by placing his right hand in front of Swick's left hip, also inhibiting his hip movement.

d. Swick feels Camarillo using forward pressure to attack his right arm so he stiff-arms Camarillo with his left hand to push him out of attacking position. If Camarillo falls back to armlock Swick's right arm, he may lose position as Swick stiff-arms and pulls his elbow to the mat.

e. Instead of falling back or losing positioning due to the stiff arm, Camarillo reaches over and secures the elbow of Swick's left stiff arm. As he does so, he begins to turn his body and pulls his hips to Swick's armpit.

f. Camarillo continues to move his body counterclockwise until his hips are completely under Swick's armpit and his knees are pinched together and ready to attack.

g. From this position it is faster for Camarillo to place his right foot under Swick's head, squeeze his knees, and fall back for the armbar. By placing his hook under Swick's head, he is able to diffuse much of his bridging power and assist his speed of transition.

SNAFU MOMENT—NOT READING SIZE OR STRENGTH:

Jiu-jitsu is incredible, but the guerrilla realizes that though size and strength matter, so does speed. When the guerrilla is faced with an obviously explosive opponent, he should seek to move around that power and to use this power and explosiveness against him. In this case, misreading this would have resulted in the guerrilla on his back without the triangle with a much stronger and aggressive opponent on top.

AFTER-ACTION REPORT:

The guerrilla was prepared for the size and strong defensive grip of the opponent. The opponent was not prepared for the discomfort and speed imposed by the guerrilla. By using his weight effectively, even the smaller guerrilla could create a predictable outcome, the opponent's push. With speed, deflection, and technique, the guerrilla was able to switch arms and maintain control of the situation through to the finish.

CONFIDENTIAL INFORMATION

1 209-83-68-888

Assembling a Fire Team

FILE 004: WHAT IS A FIRE TEAM

The fire team is a guerrilla's marquee submission. It is his favorite movement, and his entire attacking game plan revolves around the entries and situational "what-if's" that govern its success. Although it is often based on body type and athleticism, it is also a choice of the budding guerrilla to decide what direction he wants to take his attacking game. While it is sometimes a choice of style, it is always predicated on function and success.

By choosing a fire team or favored submission, the guerrilla dedicates himself to being an encyclopedia of everything regarding this submission. He may not understand one hundred submissions, but he should understand one hundred ways to get to and use his fire team. For the guerrilla, this builds depth and a situational awareness that is hard to beat. While others are cycling through their mental rolodex of positions, the guerrilla has already moved forward to his next entry or counter to his fire team. This breeds faster reactions and keeps the opponent wary.

Finally, the fire team is a submission or group of submissions that can be used in practically any situation against any type of opponent. It combines well with other submissions and it gives the guerrilla his personal mastery over jiu-jitsu. The fire team is always the guerrilla's "ace up his sleeve."

SECTION ONE: Assembling a Fire Team

When assembling a fire team for the first time, the guerrilla needs to first ensure that he has spent enough time grappling to understand and to have been exposed to many different submissions. He needs to feel which submission is his individual highest percentage and from which situation and against what type and quality of opponent he is most successful. Once this is established, he should look at his own build, gait, and natural attributes of flexibility and strength to see if this is the best movement to pursue.

As a general rule of thumb, longer guerrillas favor triangle entries though shorter guerrillas have a tighter finish, stronger guerrillas favor chokes and upper-body dominant submissions, and those with strong lower body strength often love the omoplata and armbar.

For SUBJECT CAMARILLO, throughout the years of training first in judo and then in jiu-jitsu and MMA, the armbar has been king for its speed, dedication, and versatility. Section One is an inspirational showcase of one man's total and complete dedication to his fire team.

HUNTING THE ARMBAR FROM CLOSED GUARD

- Always understand the value of using your knees, hips and grips to keep your opponent in a broken posture.
- Use "backstop grips" that trap your opponent's arm at the triceps, preventing him from easily powering his arm backward in defense.
- The closed guard armbar should be able to attack either forward or rear arm.
- Bring your hips to the opponent's armpit while you pull his arm to you.
- Develop a strong pulling action to keep your opponent's arm in the attacking range—forward and across the center line.
- Learn to beat the hand that controls your hips. Frustrate this hand and then attack the exposed arm.
- The closed guard armbar can be attacked against postured opponents and broken down opponents as well. The real point is to attack continuously.

SITREP 4.1 - CLOSED GUARD - PLATFORM ARMBAR

The closed guard platform armbar is a staple at most jiu-jitsu academies for good reason. It teaches good fundamental hip movement, body control, how to set up a proper attack angle, and a mechanical approach to the finishing game. For the guerrillas that choose other submissions, the lesson is still the same. When building a fire team from the bottom up, the starting gate is always with the fundamental techniques. There is no need to advance to difficult movements until a high measure of success has been achieved with fundamentals.

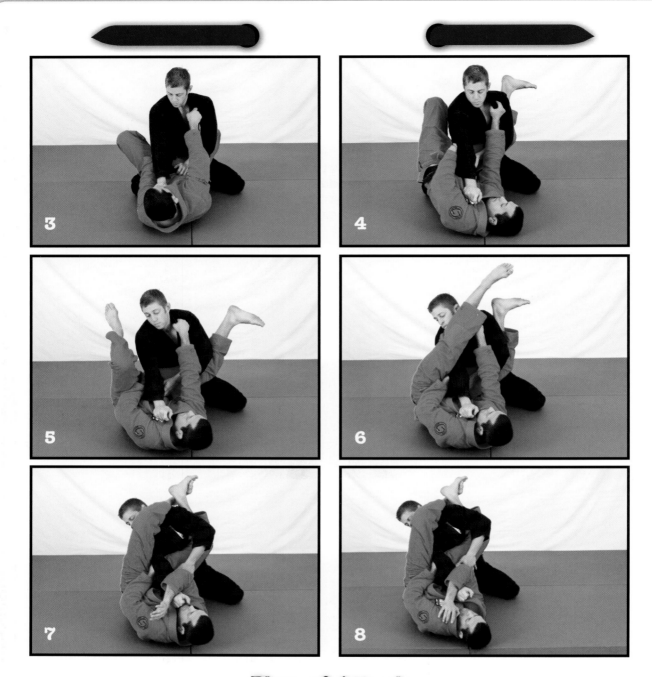

Plan of Attack:

a. Beginning from the closed guard position, SUBJECT CAMA-RILLO has his right hand on the collar and left hand on the triceps of the lead arm of CONTACT DARCY, MATTHEW. To beat Darcy's strong posture, Camarillo places his left foot on Darcy's hip, making sure his knee is pinched inward for control.

b. In one explosive movement, Camarillo lifts his hips upward, thrusting his hips into Darcy's armpit while executing a long pull with his triceps-controlling hand. As he does this, Camarillo pushes his right leg into Darcy's left armpit and swivels into a more perpendicular angle of attack.

c. Without letting his hips drop, Camarillo throws his left leg over Darcy's head. Camarillo does not release either grip on the collar or sleeve.

d. Darcy does not counter forward, believing he can pull upward and out or that Camarillo will lose strength in his attack. Camarillo does not. He locks his feet and hugs the exposed wrist with his right elbow. As he bridges his hips upward, Darcy is forced to tap.

AFTER-ACTION REPORT:

The starting point for any fire team, from any submission, is always in the fundamental techniques. The platform armbar is a good example of this methodology. Nowhere in this movement does SUBJECT CAMARILLO abandon control for flash. Instead, his focus is on grip control, understanding the exposure of the forward arm, hip elevation and creating a perpendicular angle, and finishing the tight armbar when off the back.

Again, these fundamentals are absolutely essential to a successful fire team and should be built in every possible position.

SITREP 4.2 - CLOSED GUARD - KICKSHIFT ARMBAR

SITREPs 4.1 and 4.2 take different actions for the same result. Both have the same goal of bringing the guerrilla's hips to his opponent's armpit to finish the juji gatame armbar. SITREP 4.2 focuses on base disruption to create exposure for the finish. The guerrilla keeps this tenet close to his heart whenever he is training or competing: Kuzushi (the Japanese term for off-balancing) is key. Through off-balancing, the guerrilla gains the arm exposure that he needs to get to his fire team.

Plan of Attack:

a. Like SITREP 4.1, SUBJECT CAMARILLO is in the closed guard with CONTACT DARCY, MATTHEW on top and in good posture. This time, Camarillo notices that Darcy has his knees spread wide for a stronger base and he takes advantage of this by gripping the inside of Darcy's knee with his right hand while his left hand secures the triceps of Darcy's lead arm.

b. In one motion Camarillo opens his legs and stiff-arms with his right arm to move his hips toward Darcy's exposed right arm. As he pushes, Camarillo also uses his foot on Darcy's hip to thrust his own hip upward into Darcy's armpit.

c. Continuing the push, Camarillo throws his left leg in a wide clockwise arc until it passes to the front of Darcy. Camarillo lets this momentum carry both his hips and head to align in a perpendicular angle to Darcy. Once here, Camarillo does not release the grip because Darcy would assuredly pull his arm free.

d. Unsatisfied, Camarillo pushes Darcy's leg further away to break his base forward and destabilize him. Momentarily, Darcy cannot find his balance.

e. While Darcy catches his balance, Camarillo clamps down with his left leg, secures Darcy's wrist with his left elbow and explosively thrusts his hips upward for the finish.

SNAFU MOMENT:

As with all armlocks, the point of defense is important. With the guerrilla in such a hips-high position, the triangle choke should be an easy transition if the opponent removes his arm, and the spin under juji gatame will be a great counterattack if the opponent manages to push forward at the end.

AFTER-ACTION REPORT:

The guerrilla understands that his opponent will reliably resist—always. With this in mind, he knows that to be successful he has to move to the attack, and in order to do so, he has to off-balance and use this principle of kuzushi whenever possible. His opponent will rarely just give him the submission in the easiest fashion, but to make the difficult seem simple, he uses kuzushi. To make the heavy feel light, he uses kuzushi. To make the coordinated feel clumsy, he uses kuzushi. Kuzushi, kuzushi, kuzushi.

SITREP 4.3 - MOUNTAIN CLIMBING ARMBAR

The mountain climbing armbar is an excellent example of using the opponent's action against him. In this case, the guerrilla is prepared for his opponent to stand to break the guard; in fact, his opponent should stand, because staying on his knees should feel far too perilous. With this knowledge intact, the guerrilla keeps his opponent's posture broken even when he stands, setting up for a simple and high-percentage climbing armbar attack.

Plan of Attack:

a. SUBJECT CAMARILLO is using the closed guard against CONTACT DARCY, MATTHEW. Darcy has strong posture with staggered grips and Camarillo has chosen to control both Darcy's triceps with both his grips.

b. In this situation, Darcy has chosen to stand up in hopes of avoiding Camarillo's marquee maneuver: the juji gatame armbar. Unfortunately for him, Camarillo has pulled on the grips as Darcy stood, forcing him into a bent-over posture.

c. To keep Darcy's posture broken and to set up his attack, Camarillo climbs his closed guard higher to Darcy's shoulders. This puts weight on Darcy and prevents him from looking upward.

d.. Before Darcy can even think of retreating to his knees, Camarillo hugs under Darcy's leg with his right hand and locks his left leg over Darcy's right shoulder.

e. Camarillo never wastes time or lets a moment pass him by. He immediately locks his left leg over Darcy's head, secures his arm with his left elbow, and skyrockets his hips upward for the finish.

SNAFU MOMENT:

Once the shoulder is locked, the opponent is in a lot of trouble. If he returns to both knees on the mat, he is still exposed to the armlock. In fact, this position keeps the guerrilla at a perpendicular angle and the arm never leaves the attack zone. Just be sure to prevent the opponent from stacking forward and the easy armbar once again goes to the guerrilla.

AFTER-ACTION REPORT:

The heart of SITREP 4.3 is understanding that the closed guard is not a comfortable place to be when fighting an aggressive guerrilla guard player. The opponent wants nothing to do with it and will fight to get out of range of the attacks. When the opponent tries to stand to escape, the guerrilla always opts to keep the opponent where he can attack. He does this by keeping his opponent's posture broken forward as he tries to go upright. A broken posture on the feet is just as bad as broken posture from the knees and it should be attacked with an equal amount of zeal.

SITREP 4.4 - LUMBERJACK SWEEP TO ARMBAR

As will be discussed later in this chapter, the fire team should always use easy combinations that make sense when leading to the finish. This is a preview to that section that fits in nicely with SITREP 4.3. Whenever a guerrilla attacks a lumberjack sweep, his opponent is faced with very few good options: escape the mount or fight to get to his knees. The problem for him is that fighting to get to his knees will often lead to an easy armbar as in SITREP 4.4.

Plan of Attack:

a. SUBJECT CAMARILLO is operating from the closed guard with CONTACT DARCY, MATTHEW on top and in good posture with his hands staggered for base. Camarillo is controlling both of Darcy's arms with end of the sleeve grips.

b. As in SITREP 4.3, Darcy decides to stand to avoid attack. As he lifts upward, Camarillo switches his right hand to a two-on-one grip on Darcy's right sleeve.

c. Next, Camarillo circles his left arm under Darcy's right leg. Camarillo does not only reach with his arm, but he lunges his entire body toward Darcy's leg.

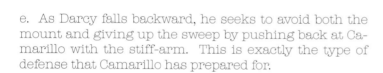

d. Camarillo pulls himself to Darcy's leg while driving his hips toward Darcy's knee to disrupt his balance and topple him backward.

e. As Darcy falls backward, he seeks to avoid both the mount and giving up the sweep by pushing back at Camarillo with the stiff-arm. This is exactly the type of defense that Camarillo has prepared for.

f. As Darcy stiff-arms, Camarillo climbs his hips high into Darcy's armpit and faces downward to the mat. Camarillo is no longer concerned with being pushed back into the guard.

g. Camarillo secures Darcy's left arm with his right arm and slides his right shin over Darcy's neck and head.

h. Once his right knee has passed over Darcy's head, Camarillo pinches it toward his left, pulls Darcy's arm to his body and drives his hips toward Darcy's flank for the finish. Darcy is forced to tap from a hyperextended left elbow.

SNAFU MOMENT:

If the opponent rolls out of this armbar, both the angle of the arm and the hooked foot behind his head will serve to roll the opponent to his back where he can be finished from a face-up juji gatame. Of course, this movement should be attacked expeditiously to keep the opponent from driving the guerrilla to his back in defense.

AFTER-ACTION REPORT:

By attacking the sweep, the guerrilla has created quite the dilemma for his opponent. Now, instead of defending the guard attacks he has two unenviable problems in front of him—either he accepts the mount and begins thinking of some type of escape plan or he pushes away and tries to fight to his knees. By choosing to fight now, he has sealed his fate as it leads directly into SITREP 4.4's armbar. This is just one of many submission pitfalls that the guerrilla creates while fool-proofing his fire team.

HUNTING ARMBARS FROM THE OPEN GUARD

- The same rules apply from the closed guard armbar when transferred to the open guard armbar, but often a much larger distance has to be crossed between the hips and the armpit.
- Use bent knees and high hips from guards such as the spider and De la Riva to keep the hips in a close attacking range.
- Constantly disrupt your opponent's balance to make him "catch" his weight, then attack his exposed arm.
- Develop grip and pulling strength not unlike a judo player to keep the opponent's arm in attack range and to straighten his arm for the attack.
- There is a greater range of hip movement in the open guard compared to the closed guard. Use this for speed and constant arm attacks.

SITREP 4.5 - SPIDER ROLLING JUJI GATAME

Regardless of the situation, the guerrilla always breaks grips and attacks the exposed limb. The open guard is no different. The spider guard is the focal point for SITREP 4.5, and through the combined use of grip control, hip movement, and the legs as a device to break grips, the attacker is able to expose the arm of his otherwise defensive opponent. However, just as important to the fire team is seizing the opportunity and finishing the instant upon recognition of the exposed arm.

Plan of Attack:

a. SUBJECT CAMARILLO is operating in the spider guard with his foot on the right biceps of CONTACT DARCY, MATTHEW. Camarillo's right knee is inside of Darcy's arm while Darcy keeps his right knee upward for base and to defend against a possible triangle choke. This gives Darcy a degree of comfort in his defense and Camarillo is about to disrupt this notion.

b. In one motion, Camarillo pulls Darcy's left sleeve to his body while kicking his right knee down to break the grip. Then, he whips his leg counterclockwise in front of Darcy's face. Camarillo pushes off with his foot on Darcy's biceps to help propel his leg around.

c. Camarillo momentarily arrives in the facedown juji gatame position and yet he still maintains control over Darcy's right arm with both his foot on the biceps and sleeve grip.

d. Camarillo rolls to his right shoulder and then releases the spider grip as his knees pinch together to secure Darcy's arm. Once more, Camarillo finishes with his flank-facing juji gatame.

AFTER-ACTION REPORT:

From the spider and open guards, one of the easiest ways to get to any attack is off of a grip break. By pulling at the sleeve and kicking the leg, an irresistible force is created that can blow through even the strongest grip. Then, by utilizing the continued pulling action, the arm is exposed for the armbar, triangle, kimura, or omoplata.

As for the submission, the guerrilla must minimize the time between recognition and submission to best take advantage of the situation. This comes through a combination of drilling and situational awareness.

SITREP 4.6 - SPIDER - MARGARIDA ARMBAR

The Margarida style armbar, regularly used by jiu-jitsu great Fernando "Margarida" Pontes, was in existence well before Margarida's time and it surely will exist long after. This classic submission from closed guard expertly uses four points of contact by the bottom guerrilla (both arms gripping and both feet pressing on the body and arms) to isolate the arm for the submission. By doubling a two-on-one grip, the guerrilla ensures that his opponent cannot easily remove his arm. To break his opponent's posture, he pushes his foot on his opponent's hip, and to prevent him from using his arm to defend, the guerrilla keeps his other foot on the opponent's biceps. From this great control comes an easy submission. As with most grappling, if you take the time to control the position, the submission comes far easier.

Plan of Attack:

a. SITREP 4.6 opens with SUBJECT CAMARILLO already having moved from spider guard control with both hands on the sleeves to a two-on-one sleeve control spider guard against CONTACT DARCY, MATTHEW. Camarillo pushes with his feet as he pulls on Darcy's sleeve to keep Darcy's posture broken forward. Darcy grabs Camarillo's inside right knee to gain some semblance of control.

b. Needing a better arm control for the inevitable armbar, Camarillo grips Darcy's right triceps with his left hand. Camarillo continues to pull with both grips while pushing with his legs, always careful not to push too far or lock his legs to set up Darcy's guard pass.

c. Camarillo does not like Darcy's left hand controlling his knee, so he circles his right foot counterclockwise, placing the arch of his foot on Darcy's biceps. Now that Camarillo is in the foot-on-the-hip spider guard, anytime Darcy circles his hand to break a grip, Camarillo will do the same to regain control.

d. Using both his foot on the biceps and his foot-on-the-hip as a platform, Camarillo lifts his hips high into Darcy's armpit. Throughout the bridging movement, Camarillo continues to pull on Darcy's sleeve with double-arm control to keep his arm in attack range.

e. The triangle is sprung as Camarillo shoots his right leg over Darcy's left shoulder. In a coordinated effort, Camarillo switches his right hand to Darcy's left leg to assist in pulling his hips perpendicular as his left grip hugs Darcy's wrist.

f. Keeping his hips high, Camarillo swings his left leg over Darcy's face to finish in the juji gatame submission. As usual, Camarillo does not delay and goes for the immediate submission.

SNAFU MOMENT—THE OPPONENT LIFTS HIS ELBOW HIGH:

Sometimes when the guerrilla has his foot on the opponent's hip, his opponent fears the triangle and keeps his elbow high (foot on the biceps arm) to hide from the triangle. In this situation, the opponent is actually signaling the guerrilla to go for the standard armbar with the leg under the arm. If the opponent becomes wary of this attack and drops his elbow to prevent that armbar, he will then go back to the triangle armbar attack.

AFTER-ACTION REPORT:

The Margarida or foot-on-the-hip spider guard efficiently controls the opponent within the closed guard. This movement is all about range. By keeping the opponent broken down forward with his arm jutting forward, the guerrilla is able to easily use the power of his lower body to get to the triangle armbar finish. This is a great position and situation for those who use the armbar, triangle, or kimura as their personal Fire Team.

SITREP 4.7 - DE LA RIVA LIFTING ARMBAR

SITREP 4.7 showcases the use of momentum combined with off-balancing to create exposure. In this case, the De la Riva is an excellent guard position to load the opponent up by pulling him over the guard as the guerrilla scoots his body deeper underneath his center of balance. From here, limb isolation and leg extension work together to project the opponent into a sweep. Again, this creates a dilemma for the person being swept—choose to accept the sweep and be rolled to your back and a possible mounted position or resist by posting your arms and deal with the possible game ending submission. The guerrilla prepares for this and is prepared for victory.

Plan of Attack:

a. SUBJECT CAMARILLO is in the seated open guard with CONTACT DARCY, MATTHEW kneeling with a dropped knee in front of him. Camarillo is gripping with a collar and sleeve control and Darcy has taken up a mirrored grip.

b. Camarillo propels himself forward by pulling with his heels as he hops his rear close to Darcy's right foot. At the same time, Camarillo puts his right foot on Darcy's hip. This large jump inside creates more leverage for Camarillo as he loads Darcy up on top of him.

c. Next, Camarillo makes an outside, or De la Riva, hook with his left shin and foot. Camarillo is careful to keep his knee pinched inward to control the leg and inhibit Darcy's defense. At this point, Camarillo nudges Darcy backward just enough to force Darcy to resist back into him.

d. As Camarillo senses the resistance, he immediately pulls with his sleeve and lapel grip while lifting with his hook. This combined with Darcy's forward motion, propels Darcy over the top of Camarillo and makes him feel much lighter.

e. In a flash, Camarillo leg-lifts Darcy into the air. While Darcy is airborne, Camarillo turns his grips counterclockwise and swings his left leg over Darcy's head.

f. The steering motion combined with the leg swing brings Darcy back to his knees in the armbar position.

g. As Camarillo presses with his legs, Darcy loses his balance and is forced to tap from the juji gatame position. In a case where the opponent retains his balance, he will be attacked with the juji gatame from the guard.

SNAFU MOMENT—RHYTHM AND TIMING:

Without a doubt, this type of armbar relies on rhythm and timing for the guerrilla. This move will take a lot of practice and should be practiced with regularity in sparring and drilling to ensure that both your hands and your hips are moving in unison. Only then will it be easy enough to execute against a fully resisting opponent.

AFTER-ACTION REPORT:

Guerrilla attacks rely on creating a series of bad decisions. By getting underneath the opponent and sweeping him up into the air, the opponent is limited to making bad decisions, none of which are particularly positive. He can accept the sweep or post his hands and be armbarred. Now, many would opt to post their hands believing they can escape the submission, but a guerrilla who channels his entire game around the armbar will welcome this and is prepared (as seen in section 4 of this chapter) to finish instantly.

SITREP 4.8 - DE LA RIVA ALL-THE-WAY ARMBAR

SITREP 4.8 is the "what-if" to SITREP 4.7's De la Riva armbar attack. In this case, the what-if that the guerrilla is prepared for is base. What if the opponent lands in posture and is prepared to defend the submission? Simply, he continues his momentum and stays with the arm through to the finish. The all-the-way armbar is a great example of focusing on the finish, being dedicated to the attack, and giving way to force to get to the fire team.

Plan of Attack:

a. As with SITREP 4.7, SUBJECT CAMARILLO has progressed from a seated guard to a De la Riva guard against CONTACT DARCY, MATTHEW. Darcy has his left knee dropped to the mat and is resisting forward against Camarillo's pushing action.

b. Using his outside De la Riva hook and foot-on-the-hip combined with a strong pulling action of his grips, Camarillo is able to boost Darcy into the air. With Camarillo's center directly under Darcy, this is easily accomplished.

c. Camarillo continues to boost Darcy upward while Darcy attempts to balance with his hands. As soon as Camarillo feels Darcy using this type of athleticism and counterbalancing, he allows his hips to further follow Darcy.

d. As Darcy falls back to his feet, Camarillo moves his hips to the outside and latches onto the armbar position. This time, however, Darcy has managed to regain his positioning and is pressuring forward into Camarillo in a stacking counter.

e. Staying with the armlock is not new to Camarillo so he reaches his right hand in front of Darcy's right leg while his left hand hugs Darcy's right wrist. Camarillo begins pulling with his right arm to bring his head toward Darcy's right hip.

f. As Camarillo pulls his head toward Darcy's right hip, Darcy is forced out of balance to his front right corner. This causes Darcy to fall headfirst onto the mat.

g. To finish, Camarillo controls Darcy's arm with both arms and bridges his hips into Darcy's elbow. It is important, however, that Camarillo stays on his side instead of face down to effect a greater range on his bridging motion and to preemptively defend the possibility of Darcy jumping to the other side in defense.

SNAFU MOMENT—FINISHING ON THE SIDE VS FACEDOWN:

In this situation, finishing on the side allows the guerrilla to follow his opponent if the opponent manages to jump to the other side. This will force the opponent to fall to his back as he goes to the other side. Otherwise, if he attacks a facedown armbar, he could lose the submission and end up on the bottom if the opponent executes the same defense.

AFTER-ACTION REPORT:

The guerrilla should practice SITREPs 4.7 and 4.8 together to ensure that he is capable of realizing when he should continue his momentum and flow to the hips-facing armbar. In this way, there will be little or no shock when the dexterous opponent manages to land on his feet and renew his defense; there will only be attack and the continued path toward the finish. Of course, he should also have his game built around pushing his opponent to his back, as in SITREP 4.7, because this is a top position, but he must always seek total preparation as well.

ARMBAR HUNTING WHILE GUARD-PASSING

- In most cases, the arm to be attacked is the near-side arm on the same side to which the guerrilla is passing.
- For simple arm attacks, combine knee-on-belly-style armbars whenever the opponent pushes with a stiff-arm.
- Losing the armpit and/or near-side leg control can lead to reversal, so stay tight and firm with the controls.
- Pressure and pace often lead to the arm-exposing stiff-arm—keep this in mind at all times!
- Use your hips and posture to pull the arm straight.

SITREP 4.9 - PASSING: ARMBAR OFF GUARD DEFENSE

Most think of submissions from dominant top or guard positions and not off the guard pass. To them, the guard is only a danger and is there to be passed. Guerrillas think differently and choose to attack their fire team whenever possible. In SITREP 4.9, the armbar is attacked against the defensive guard. This is not a lightning fast armbar. Instead, it is built on patience, pressure, and body placement. Then, it is finished through an explosiveness that can only be created from leverage.

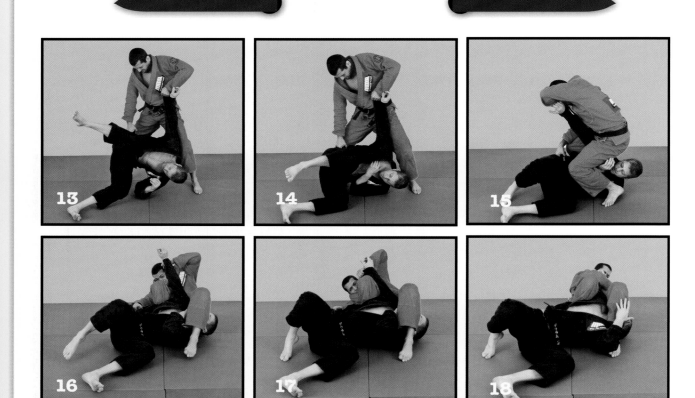

Plan of Attack:

a. SUBJECT CAMARILLO is approaching the open guard of CONTACT DARCY, MATTHEW. Camarillo is controlling both of Darcy's feet to prevent him from easily moving them into control positions. As always, Camarillo is thinking of his armbar attacks.

b. In one motion, Camarillo pushes both of Darcy's heels toward his rear, pressing his feet into his body. This weakens Darcy's legs, as their optimal angle for attack and defense is closer to ninety degrees. As Camarillo pressures the legs, he goes to his knees, pressing his hips into Darcy's right shin.

c. At this point, Camarillo grabs Darcy's belt with his right hand making sure his right forearm helps to lock Darcy's right leg to his body. As he is making this grip, Camarillo also grips the belt with his left hand for greater control.

d. With Darcy's left leg free, he begins to circle it clockwise to defend the position. He also tries to grip Camarillo's collar to stiff-arm him away. This is what Camarillo is looking for and grips Darcy's right sleeve as it is offered.

e. Darcy completes his defensive move by circling his left leg in front of Camarillo's face to defend the position. Camarillo is not concerned by this as he simply tucks his left elbow in front of Darcy's shin for control.

f. Surprising Darcy, Camarillo jumps to his feet. Still, Darcy believes that his left leg is enough to impede Camarillo from passing his guard.

Assembling a Fire Team

g. In the same motion, Camarillo stands all the way to posture while he pulls Darcy's sleeve and belt toward him. This forces Darcy's leg to swing effortlessly away from Camarillo and opens up Darcy's right side to the guard pass.

h. Thinking like a guerrilla, Camarillo forgoes the pass because he is in complete control of Darcy's right arm. Instead, he pulls the arm upward and steps over Darcy's head with his left foot.

i. With both legs in position, Camarillo falls to his back, pinches his knees together, and forces Darcy to submit from the juji gatame armbar.

AFTER-ACTION REPORT:

While the opponent is thinking he has blocked the guard pass with his leg as a block, the guerrilla is patiently getting his belt and sleeve control so he can spring to the attack. There cannot be a greater difference in mindsets than the two present in this situation. One is content with survival and defense while the other is hunting, hungry, and progressive. In other words, one is waiting for the end and the other is pursuing it.

SITREP 4.10 - PASSING: SIT-UP GUARD TO ARMBAR

SITREP 4.10 is an incredible armbar that again takes advantage of the surprise that accompanies most submissions off of the guard pass. In this situation, the guerrilla understands that the opponent is so fixated on holding the leg and fighting for the single-leg reversal that his best plan is to remove his leg to the outside to diffuse the power of the grip instead of working on the grip itself. Once successful, the opponent's previously advantageous grip becomes his tombstone, as the grip becomes the arm under attack. In fact, due to this grip, the mount, the triangle, and the armbar all become available. For disciplined guerrillas, the focus is not so much on a steadfast grip or hold, but on the submission.

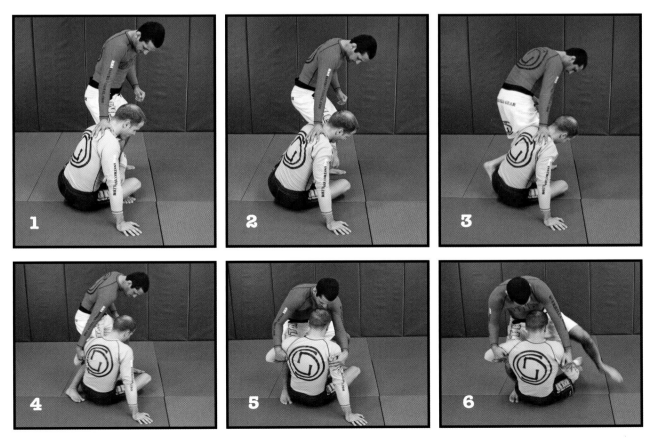

Plan of Attack:

a. SUBJECT CAMARILLO is attempting to pass the seated guard of CONTACT FERRISS, TIMOTHY. Ferriss has already pulled himself to a good attacking position on the outside of Camarillo's knee and is attempting to push Camarillo forward, knees first into the mat. Camarillo has countered by driving his knee to the outside into Ferriss's abdomen and pressing on his left shoulder for control.

b. With his knee still pointing at Ferriss, Camarillo chambers his right leg and begins to circle it clockwise out from between Ferriss's legs. This is easily accomplished as Ferriss was too focused on Camarillo's knee pressure and shoulder control to maintain a firm grip on the leg.

c. As Camarillo completes the escape of his right leg, he firmly stomps on the mat next to Ferriss's left hip and pulls up his left triceps. By pulling up his arm, Camarillo makes it incredibly difficult for Ferriss to return to his back to regain the guard and exposes his arm for the coming attack.

d. Continuing his pull on the right triceps, Camarillo then grips under Ferriss's left arm to do the same. As he does so, Camarillo hops his left leg clear over Ferriss's right leg and arm, arriving in a near triangle position. At this point, Camarillo increases his effort to pull Ferriss's left arm to him.

e. Camarillo continues to pull the arm deep under his armpit as he falls to his left thigh and hip across Ferriss's upper torso. Camarillo pinches his right knee toward Ferriss's shoulder to maintain control of the arm while his right arm assists by acting as an overhooking clamp.

f. Camarillo pinches his knees together. At this point, many will tap from the pressure, but in this case, Ferriss is very flexible and strong and has yet to submit.

g. To finish, Camarillo hugs Ferriss's left leg in a classic leg-side armbar, crosses his right leg over Ferriss's head for added control, and finishes with the juji gatame armbar.

SNAFU MOMENT—UNDER-THE-ARM ESCAPES:

When attacking the under-the-arm-style finish of the juji gatame, the submission comes on strong and fast, making it difficult for your opponent to defend. Still, it is important to use leg-side SAP control to ensure that he does not roll away from the submission. Though a strong clamp can minimize this, there is always the chance of rollout against an equally strong-willed opponent. In addition, the guerrilla is always prepared to move to the triangle or triangle/armbar if his opponent drives into him.

AFTER-ACTION REPORT:

The guerrilla understands that getting rid of the arm grip around the leg will be far more difficult than removing the foot from the control. By seeking the path of least resistance, the guerrilla creates a "freeway" opening that shoots straight through to the armbar, kimura, triangle, omoplata, mount, etc. Again, he must seize the opportunity and act upon recognition. Preparation should always lead to action instead of hesitation.

SITREP 4.11 - PASSING: NEGATIVE SIT-UP PASS TO ARMBAR

The negative pass to armbar is an excellent combination with SITREP 4.10. In this situation, the opponent pulls his entire body to the outside of the knee-under control. This eliminates the necessary angle to turn the foot out for the guerrilla and threatens the back and single leg. However, the guerrilla always follows the momentum of the fight, albeit with a strong attack! For SITREP 4.11, the single-leg may be a threat, but the negative-side armbar is exposed for those who dare to win!

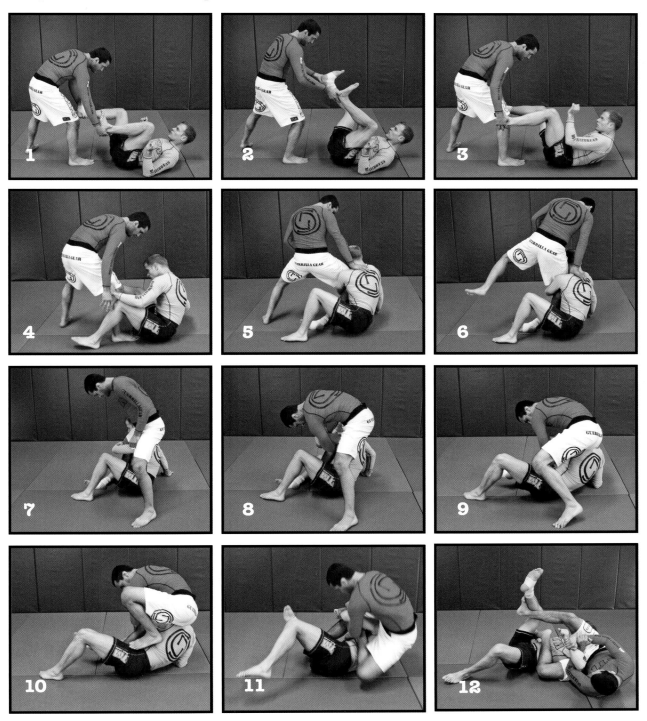

Assembling a Fire Team

Plan of Attack:

a. SUBJECT CAMARILLO is approaching the open guard of CONTACT FERRISS, TIMOTHY. As always, Camarillo does not delay in establishing control of Ferriss's heels. At this point, Ferriss is focused solely on defending these grips and has been momentarily taken out of his previous mindset.

b. Without delay, Camarillo pushes Ferriss's legs overhead and waits for him to rock back in defense. As Ferriss falls into the first trap, Camarillo steps inside of his seated guard. Ferriss does not wait and grabs the single-leg to gain advantage and attack.

c. However, Camarillo realizes that the single-leg is the most common reaction and is already cross-stepping backward with his left leg before Ferriss can execute a sweep or takedown. Due to his perfect timing, Camarillo does not have to wait for Ferriss to establish a stronger defense of the backward cross-step.

d. Having reached Ferriss's left side, Camarillo now focuses on the arm by securing a figure-four kimura lock on Ferriss's exposed (from holding the single-leg) left leg. Camarillo's right leg is still technically inside of the guard, but Camarillo has little concern for it; he is completely focused on the finish.

e. To break Ferriss's posture and initiate the final sequence, Camarillo jumps his left foot to Ferriss's left hip and drops his rear to Ferriss's left shoulder. This collapses Ferriss toward the mat and sets him up for the submission.

f. As Camarillo falls to his back, he slides a belt line hook with his left leg and uses his right foot as a hook to steer Ferriss away from his trapped arm. This keeps Ferriss planted to his back where it is far more difficult to defend.

g. Ferriss locks the triangle on Camarillo's right leg, but it does not matter. Camarillo's right leg blocks Ferriss's right arm from making a proper defense and his triangle makes it impossible to roll to either side to escape. Camarillo stretches Ferriss's arm for the finish.

SNAFU MOMENT—DO NOT EXCHANGE:

The guerrilla does not exchange. He does not trade one favorable movement for another favorable movement. In SITREP 4.10, the guerrilla makes sure to advance his game every single time the opponent counters to catch up to him. He does not allow him to catch up and then execute his own attack. The goal is to keep the opponent one breath from drowning and not treading water.

AFTER-ACTION REPORT:

By cross-stepping backward, the guerrilla does two things at once: He eliminates the chance of having his back taken or of being taken down to his knees and he once more exposes the near-side armbar for the attack. As with SITREP 4.10, the elbow control after the cross-step is critical to finding success with this submission because a lack of control may lead to a guard recovery or reversal. So for the guerrilla to try to fall into the submission, he must also believe he will get to the near-side elbow at any cost!

SITREP 4.12 - MANA STORM PASS TO ARMBAR

The Mana Storm armbar is a game of cat and mouse for the guerrilla that includes predictive and psychological elements that will be seen in chapter 7, and it builds upon the previous SITREPs. At the heart of this technique is the chase. By dictating the chase and setting the pace, the guerrilla is able to predict and capitalize on the exuberance of the opponent to maintain and reverse the position, leading to not only back exposure, but the game-finishing submission.

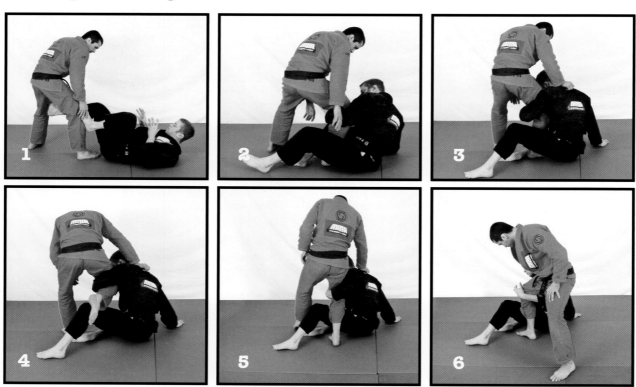

Plan of Attack:

a.   SUBJECT CAMARILLO approaches the open guard of CON-TACT DARCY, MATTHEW.   As always, he is controlling Darcy's feet to ensure that he initiates the passing offense.

b. Camarillo then inserts his foot in between Darcy's legs and Darcy sits forward into a seated guard, hugging Camarillo's right leg. To defend the position, Camarillo points his knee toward Darcy's abdomen and pushes Darcy's shoulders with his right hand. This forces Darcy to exert more effort to keep upright and maintain control.

c. As with SITREP 4.10, Camarillo circle-steps his right leg out of the guard and is forcing Darcy to catch up to him.

d. A fraction of a second after circling his right leg free, Camarillo cross-steps his left leg back so that both feet are on the left side of Darcy. At this point, Camarillo does not drop to the side. Instead, he stays upright and is prepared for Darcy's immediate reaction.

e. Darcy explosively turns toward Camarillo and grabs his leg with an inside single-leg. Always prepared, Camarillo pushes Darcy's head downward with his right forearm and evades Darcy's attack by stepping back with his left leg toward Darcy's back.

f. Camarillo then takes advantage of Darcy's posted arm from the previous frame. He understands that Darcy needs this arm pushing off the mat to prevent himself from falling into a worse position, so Camarillo uses that space to underhook the arm with his left arm and insert his left foot underneath.

g. As Camarillo finishes inserting his left hook, he uses that momentum to roll himself onto his left shoulder and then back. While Darcy is focused on the roll and back-take, Camarillo sinks in a tight figure-four lock on Darcy's left arm and locks his feet together in a modified triangle/belt line control from the back.

h. With his right arm trapped by Camarillo's locked right leg, Darcy is unable to defend the submission, and Camarillo pulls the arm to him for the juji gatame armbar.

SNAFU MOMENT:

If the guerrilla sets up the chase, he must understand how to counter with his back and forward steps in order to prevent the takedown. He also should understand fatigue and other psychological factors. If he slows against a well-conditioned opponent, he may be reversed, so constant motion is key to success!

AFTER-ACTION REPORT:

By staying ahead of the opponent, the guerrilla is able to control the chase. As with any chase, he must keep going as soon as his opponent commits to his countermeasure. Failure only leads to either neutrality or a disadvantage. The only way to stay ahead is to keep pushing ahead. It is vital that guerrillas establish this mindset to keep pressing toward the mission's end goal—to keep pressing on to their preferred fire team.

HUNTING ARMBARS FROM SIDE CONTROL & NORTH-SOUTH

- Always attempt to isolate the near-side arm before attacking near- or far-side armbars.
- Deflect the power of pressing stiff-arms and pulling over-the-shoulder grips with hips and shoulders to clear any defense for the armbar.
- Use your entire body to isolate the arm for attack and not just your arms.
- Develop the ability to walk from side control to side control before jumping into spinning armbars.
- Always understand the relationship between the armbars and the other powerhouse submission from side control and north-south: the kimura.
- While transitioning with a side control or north-south armbar, put pressure on the elbow joint throughout the movement.

SITREP 4.13 - SIDE CONTROL: NEAR-SIDE ARMBAR

SITREP 4.13 takes the near-side armbar control that is important to all submissions and top control and takes it to a new level. Instead of simply isolating the arm and returning to the control which is very common in grappling and jiu-jitsu academies, the guerrilla makes the most use of his hip and arm deflection by following the momentum through to the finish.

Plan of Attack:

a. SUBJECT CAMARILLO is in the kuzure kesa gatame top position of CONTACT DARCY, MATTHEW. For Camarillo, this is a preferable judo-style pin when compared to the kesa gatame or scarf-hold because he retains control and does not provide his opponent with an opportunity to take his back. Camarillo controls with hip pressure, a strong pulling motion on Darcy's right triceps, and an underhook of Darcy's left arm.

b. To help distribute the pulling load of Camarillo's left pulling arm, he begins to push off the mat with his left leg, driving his hips into Darcy's right triceps. This full body action is much harder for Darcy to defend and he is unable to pull his elbow back toward his body in defense.

c. Camarillo continues to drive Darcy's arm forward and then turns his body to face Darcy, using his upper body to secure Darcy's arm at the triceps. To set up the inevitable armbar, Camarillo clasps his left arm over Darcy's wrist. Without his right arm to serve as a brace, Darcy feels all of Camarillo's weight crashing into his torso. In addition, Camarillo deflects Darcy's left arm away from any practical defensive positioning.

d. Next Camarillo switches his base, stepping his left leg clear over Darcy's face. His hips continue to press Darcy's arm into his body, while his head angles toward the far-side hip for better weight distribution and to set up the armbar attack.

e. To finish, Camarillo rolls back to his left side, and arches his hips toward Darcy's head to hyperextend the right elbow joint. Camarillo continually pushes Darcy's left hand throughout to ensure that he cannot get underneath Camarillo's left leg for defense.

AFTER-ACTION REPORT:

The key to this movement is in how the guerrilla deflects the near-side defensive arm by first pulling at the elbow and then using his body to straighten the arm across his opponent's body. This is easily achieved because the guerrilla bonds his opponent's elbow to his own body. Therefore, when he straightens his body toward his opponent's hip, the arm naturally follows. Besides the arm following, the guerrilla's hips also follow making this a strong submission, especially for how it takes advantage of momentum.

SITREP 4.14 - SIDE CONTROL: SPINNING HEAD-SIDE ARMBAR

Whenever an opponent defends the side control by reaching over a shoulder to pull the opponent into a bridge or roll over, he is playing Russian roulette with his arm. The guerrilla understands this and attacks the mistakenly exposed arm every single time. Throughout SITREP 4.14, the guerrilla attacks slowly and methodically, using great hip and chest pressure to prevent hip mobility or escape. By straightening the arm throughout the transition, the guerrilla has the opponent begging for the finish at multiple junctions!

Assembling a Fire Team

Plan of Attack:

a. SUBJECT CAMARILLO is in the top side control position of CONTACT DARCY, MATTHEW. Camarillo is blocking Darcy's hips with his right hand while his left hand takes an over-the-shoulder grip. This is a classic pin that is great for immobilizing the escaping far shoulder and preventing the guard recovery. Darcy's left arm is trapped and Camarillo is moving to secure it with his left hand.

b. As Camarillo traverses to the north-south pin, he continuously blocks Darcy's hips, roadblocking Darcy from following him. On the arm side, Camarillo keeps a tight grip above the elbow while using his head to keep Darcy's arm straightened.

c. With the north-south pin secured, Camarillo can now clasp his hands together to exert further pressure on the trapped arm. Camarillo begins to set up the armbar by moving his head toward Darcy's right hip, all the while using his head to keep the arm controlled.

d. Camarillo continues to move his head toward Darcy's right flanks and then slides his rear to the mat with his pelvis underneath Darcy's armpit. He slides his left knee upward to lock the position and prevent Darcy's escape.

e. With the arm extremely outstretched, Camarillo falls toward the head side, bridges his hips upward, and completes the incredibly tight armbar.

SNAFU MOMENT—LACK OF HEAD CONTROL:

If the guerrilla fails to pin the arm using his head and neck as well as the grips, the opponent is likely to turn his hand out to escape. This situation will be covered in SITREP 4.15, though there is also an option to attack the kimura lock. As with all kimuras, proper body control is key, especially when preventing the opponent from gripping his gi or body in defense.

AFTER-ACTION REPORT:

This submission and the transition are incredibly tight and uncomfortable for the opponent. With proper hand and head placement, both the arm and the hips of the opponent are essentially immobilized and the clamp grip creates elbow hyperextension during the entire movement phase. For the guerrilla mindset, this move is of special importance; it helps the guerrilla to understand the importance of creating pain in a submission long before the finish. By doing so, he will take the focus away from the escape and away from the transition, leaving the opponent focused solely on the pain at hand.

SITREP 4.15 - SIDE CONTROL: SPINNING ARMBAR W/HOOK FOOT

Where SITREP 4.14 covers an armbar when the opponent grips over the head-side shoulder, SITREP 4.15 focuses on the spinning armbar when the grip is over the leg-side shoulder. The difference between the two is in how the guerrilla can open up more space and utilize greater speed in transitioning to the submission because he has greater control over the arm with just one arm, instead of using the head, neck, weight, and clamping grip as in SITREP 4.14.

Plan of Attack:

a. SUBJECT CAMARILLO has reached the side control of CONTACT DARCY, MATTHEW. Camarillo's right knee is across Darcy's belly while he hugs Darcy's left arm with his right arm. For stabilization and balance, Camarillo pushes off the floor with his left arm close to Darcy's head.

Assembling a Fire Team

b. Instead of circling to the other side, Camarillo swings his left leg in a clockwise arc, inserting his left foot underneath Darcy's left arm. Camarillo will momentarily have to "jump" his left hand to let the leg cross underneath it.

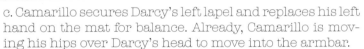

c. Camarillo secures Darcy's left lapel and replaces his left hand on the mat for balance. Already, Camarillo is moving his hips over Darcy's head to move into the armbar.

d. Spotting his landing, Camarillo places his rear where his outstretched hand was. At this point, Camarillo is already pulling against Darcy's left forearm to prevent his defense.

e. Moving to a rear-naked lock on the wrist, Camarillo focuses his entire body on hyperextending Darcy's left elbow for the submission.

SNAFU MOMENT—NOT USING THE PLANK:

The concept of planking should be on the mind of the guerrilla as he attacks his style of an armbar. If all of the guerrilla's weight is in one place and the guerrilla loses balance, he may not only lose the submission, but also the strong top control. Instead, the guerrilla must learn to blanket his weight over a greater surface area to create a sense of suffocation and stability.

AFTER-ACTION REPORT:

Whenever the opponent opens a hole between his elbow and his body or grips over the leg-side shoulder while in side control, he is susceptible to the spinning arm attack. This allows for lightning-fast transitions to the other side and creative entries into the finishing position by hooking the foot to transition straight to the submission instead of moving first to the other side and then to the submission. This attack is all about speed, compared to SITREP 4.14, which is dedicated purely to pressure, patience, and even more pressure.

SITREP 4.16 - NORTH-SOUTH: DOUBLE ARMBAR (REACTIONARY)

When arriving at the north-south position, most experienced grapplers will position themselves so that their hands and forearms are inside the attacker's arms as he reaches the pin. To evade this defense, the guerrilla focuses on the fundamentals before moving to the immediate submission. A guerrilla learns to address the defense first and then to attack. Otherwise, by attacking an opponent with strong defense the guerrilla is likely to lose position, or worse, end up in a defensive situation of his own.

Plan of Attack:

a. SUBJECT CAMARILLO is in the north-south position with CONTACT DARCY, MATTHEW, in a bottom defensive posture. Both of Darcy's elbows are inside of Camarillo's, and this positioning is providing him with some space to both defend and escape.

b. To deflect Darcy's right arm, Camarillo swims his right arm counterclockwise, passing his hand toward Darcy's torso and then around to the outside, where he can lock his arm around Darcy's.

c. From here, Camarillo commits to the exact same action but reversed to secure Darcy's left arm. Through this process, Darcy's arms are deflected to the outside where they can be outstretched and trapped.

d. Now that he has both arms stretched and secured, Camarillo drives his head toward Darcy's legs and pinches his grips inward, creating a slight hyperextension on both elbows. Also, Camarillo steps his left foot upward to prepare for the armbar submission.

e. Camarillo continues to slide his left knee upward, making sure it is outside of Darcy's left arm. Then he moves toward the upright left knee and falls into the SAP. From this SAP Camarillo continues to grip both arms with elbow control.

f. With both arms stretched out, Darcy has no way to escape or fight the control. Camarillo continues to hold both arms, squeezes his knees together, and forces Darcy to tap from the elbow hyperextension.

SNAFU MOMENT—LOSING THE BOTTOM ARM:

The guerrilla always has options on top of options, a hallmark of *preparation*. In a case where the opponent pulls the bottom elbow free, the guerrilla should continue attacking. He should focus on the top arm now by attacking either straight arm lock submissions or omoplata/kimura shoulder locks. The guerrilla always prepares for success and his constant attacks threaten the morale of his enemies.

AFTER-ACTION REPORT:

Every guerrilla must first learn to submit an opponent who has already reached a strong defensive position. By spending time drilling and learning to beat the defense before attacking, the guerrilla learns to attack at the most opportune moment when the opponent is most vulnerable. This is showcased in SITREP 4.16, where the guerrilla takes the time to beat both defensively positioned arms before tying them both up and finishing with the preferred fire team.

SITREP 4.17 - NORTH-SOUTH: LIFTING KIMURA ARMBAR

A guerrilla attacker must also understand when to transition between positions in order to both keep the top position and transition to the best possible submission. In SITREP 4.17, the far-side underhook tells the guerrilla that the opponent seeks to hip escape and possibly get to his knees. With this in mind, the guerrilla understands that it is time to transition to the north-south to deflect the arm and to turn this underhook into a kimura-to-armbar submission combination.

Assembling a Fire Team

Plan of Attack:

a. CONTACT DARCY, MATTHEW is already trying to escape the side control of SUBJECT CAMARILLO. Darcy has managed to secure an underhook with his left hand, has pushed Camarillo away and into north-south with his right hand on the hip, and is turning as if to get to his knees. Camarillo has his elbows tight and his toes on the floor and is ready to counter with weight, position, and technique.

b. As Darcy continues to turn, his left hand becomes extremely exposed. Camarillo wraps his left hand under the elbow and secures his own right wrist, which is also clamping down on Darcy's wrist. This figure-four lock will not only set up the submission, but it also deeply limits Darcy's mobility.

c. With the lock in place, Camarillo never waits. He jumps up to his feet while pushing Darcy's own hand into his body for control. Darcy cannot move as he watches Camarillo shift toward his left side for the submission.

d. Camarillo falls to the side and is in a head-side SAP with the figure-four control. It is critical for Camarillo to continue to push the kimura lock into Darcy to prevent him from rolling over his right shoulder to escape.

e. Ready to attack the submission, Camarillo turns the kimura by swiveling his shoulders clockwise. This shoulder locks Darcy and forces him to release his defensive grip. If he resists, the torque of the movement will have a prying effect to pull his arm free.

f. With the arm now completely exposed, Camarillo only has to fall back into his standard armbar to finish Darcy.

AFTER-ACTION REPORT:

It is critical that guerrillas understand when it is time to transition to a new control position, but it is even better when the guerrilla makes this transition for the benefit of staying dominant and exposing the fight-finishing submission. For SITREP 4.17, the guerrilla moves to a north-south kimura when his opponent seeks an underhook escape from side control. This underhook can always be turned into a kimura as long as the guerrilla understands how to transition to expose the arm. Once in the position, the guerrilla can use this grip to keep the opponent pinned, and this buys him the necessary time to transition into the game-finishing armbar.

As with any top position, the budding guerrilla must take a lesson from this move—always analyze every possible escape from every pin and devise a way to transition into the fire team. This fire team essential is further discussed in section 4 of this chapter: Beating the Defense.

HUNTING ARMBARS FROM SINGLE-LEG ATTACK

- By practicing the armbar off the shot for standing armbars or from the side control transition to the knees, the guerrilla has more time and a better chance to develop the submission.
- All single-leg armbars attack the strong (near-side) arm. This is the arm that is usually stuck underneath the guerrilla.
- Do not get bowled over by the single-leg reversal or takedown. Instead, learn to effectively use the sprawl and to dominate your opponent's head. This gives the guerrilla much more time to set up the armbar transition.
- For the standing armbar, controlling the head makes for a much smaller jump to the submission.
- This is a great submission when facing strong wrestlers and MMA fighters.

SITREP 4.18 - SINGLE-LEG DEFENSE TO ROLLING KIMURA

In SITREP 4.17 the guerrilla successfully predicted the opponent's attempt to turn into the single-leg and preemptively submitted him. Though this is ideal, sometimes the opponent is too experienced or explosive and manages to get to his knees and secure the single-leg from a kneeling position. This is the situation that the guerrilla must be prepared to beat with his fire team. In SITREP 4.18, the guerrilla uses the rolling kimura not only to reverse the single-leg attack, but also to end with the armbar.

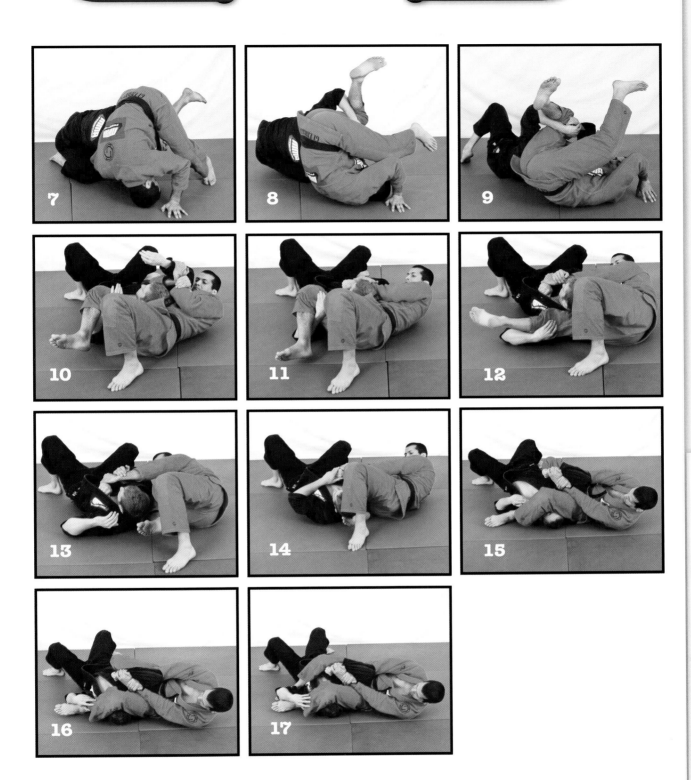

Plan of Attack:

a. SUBJECT CAMARILLO is on the top of side control with CONTACT DARCY, MATTHEW on the bottom. Camarillo has both arms on the left side of Darcy with his elbows close to Darcy's neck/ear and hip. Darcy is wisely keeping his elbows tight and hiding his arms and wrists to prevent possible arm submissions.

b. Without a cross-face or hip block to keep Darcy on his back, he bridges and then turns to his left in an attempt to reverse the position with a single-leg reversal on Camarillo's right leg. Camarillo sprawls to prevent Darcy from easily walking his knees underneath his body and to keep his arms outstretched.

c. As Darcy fights to his knees, Camarillo circles his right hand under Darcy's armpit until he can reach Darcy's right wrist. Also, Camarillo keeps his left hand on the mat for balance. At this junction Darcy still believes he will get the reversal.

d. In an instant Camarillo changes the game and rolls over his right shoulder. As he rolls, he kicks both legs to the mat. This forces Darcy to roll to his back because his single-leg attempt places his left arm between both of Camarillo's legs. His arm is essentially stuck and he has to go with Camarillo.

e. As soon as his back hits the mat, Camarillo locks a figure-four lock on Darcy's right arm. Until the lock is in place, Camarillo will keep Darcy's left arm grounded, stuck between his two legs. This will prevent Darcy from reacting by turning into Camarillo and forcing him to his back.

f. With the kimura lock or figure-four hold in place, Camarillo can now release Darcy's left arm as he hip escapes away from Darcy's head. Camarillo will continue to pressure Darcy's hand into his own midsection to prevent him from turning toward him.

g. With his hips escaped, Camarillo places his left leg over Darcy's face while his right knee slides into the armbar finishing position.

h. From this control, Camarillo can either finish with the kimura lock as he does here or move to a head-side SAP finish as in SITREP 4.16

AFTER-ACTION REPORT:

In order to execute the rolling kimura reversal, the guerrilla must make sure that the opponent continues to hug his leg and that both of his arms are secured (one by an underhook and forearm trap and the other trapped by his lower leg). This means that the opponent will be trapped once he is rolled to his back, and that the guerrilla will have more than enough time to trap the kimura lock and transition to the armbar, the back, or to the top position. This is an incredible reversal and counter to the single-leg, but it should be drilled many times prior to being put to use.

SITREP 4.19 - SINGLE-LEG DEFENSE TO TRIANGLE ARMBAR

Whether it is a transition from a kneeling single-leg as in SITREP 4.18 or a standard wrestler's shot, the guerrilla must practice single-leg defense as part of his defensive fire team repertoire. For this situation the guerrilla must put weight on the attacker's head and swing his leg to the outside to set up the triangle jump. The lower the head is pushed the easier the jump. This is also an excellent transition for guerrillas who favor triangle-based fire teams.

Plan of Attack:

a. SITREP 4.19 begins with CONTACT SWICK, MICHAEL attacking the high single-leg takedown against SUBJECT CAMARILLO. Camarillo is whizzering or overhooking with his right arm to prevent his back from being taken while pushing down on Swick's head to prevent him from posturing up.

b. While continuously pushing Swick's head away with his left "stiff" hand, Camarillo circles his right leg out in a clockwise fashion until his shin and right foot are hooked to the outside of Swick's left leg. This changes the direction of Swick's single-leg and he takes the bait, entering between Camarillo's legs for a trip-style takedown.

c. As Swick postures forward, Camarillo jumps clear over Swick's right arm into a leg triangle. This is possible because both of his arms are tied up with the single-leg attack. As he gets to the triangle, Camarillo pulls up on Darcy's left triceps to ensure a tight lock with the arm inside.

d. Camarillo's shoulders fall to the floor and inevitably Swick must follow him with broken posture. Immediately, Swick grips the belt to begin posturing out of the triangle while Camarillo grips the triceps to clear the arm for the attack.

e. Just as Camarillo clears the arm across his centerline, Swick begins to posture upward in fear of being trapped in a triangle choke. By posturing up while pushing Camarillo's hips down, he should be able to break the choke attempt.

f. Though posture breaks the triangle, it also feeds directly into Camarillo's armbar. With Swick's arm outstretched, Camarillo easily swings his leg over Swick's head and finishes with a tight juji gatame armlock against a completely upright opponent.

SNAFU MOMENT—POSTURE BREAK:

In a case where the guerrilla completely devastates his opponent's posture with his triangle jump, the guerrilla should focus on finishing the triangle choke. The guerrilla always understands that broken posture favors the suffocating triangle while upright posture breaks the triangle and feeds the arm attacks.

AFTER-ACTION REPORT:

The flying triangle armbar off the single-leg is dazzling and a definite crowd pleaser, but it is also effective. It is recommended that the guerrilla first practice standard rear breakfalls on the mat with his basic judo throws such as osoto-gari, then transition to jumping guard free falls on a crash pad, and then later jumping guard breakfalls on the mat. This will prepare him to absorb the shock of any failed landing and provide him with the fighting spirit and confidence to commit to the flying attack.

As for the triangle submission itself, the guerrilla should always finish the triangle armbar series depending on the way the opponent defends. If the opponent bends forward to stack the armbar, he essentially assists the guerrilla in locking an even tighter triangle. If he attempts to posture out of the possible triangle, he usually elongates his arm, making the armbar much easier. The tactical guerrilla should always play with this dynamic to get the finish.

HUNTING ARMBARS FROM KNEE-ON-BELLY

- All of the pointers for hunting side control armbars apply to the knee-on-belly armbar.
- Analogous to the guard and open guard, the knee-on-belly armbar usually has a farther distance to travel to the armpit than the side control. Keep your body crouched and close to the armpit to lessen this distance.
- Many armbars will become available through proper pressure—that is, making your opponent "want" to give up an arm to be finished instead of crushed. These should be drilled for rapid-fire speed with a focus on getting a shin-hook into the armbar.
- The shin-hook is often used on the leg-side arm of either the near-side armbar or far-side armbar because it is much faster than circling the leg-side leg over the body. In this case, efficiency correlates with speed.

SITREP 4.20 - KNEE-ON-BELLY: SAME-SIDE ARMBAR

When moving to the knee-on-belly position, the guerrilla must focus on how the position creates opportunities. Instead of simply sliding the knee across the belly and balancing atop a bucking opponent, the guerrilla should drive his knee vertically toward the solar plexus. This will curl the opponent as he loses the ability to lie flat and breathe comfortably and will make it far easier to isolate the near-side arm. In fact, many abdominally weak opponents will give up the arm in hopes of having the knee-on-belly torture end.

Plan of Attack:

a. SUBJECT CAMARILLO is in the knee-on-belly on top of CONTACT SWICK, MICHAEL. Camarillo is controlling Swick's right triceps and is posting his right hand on Swick's left shoulder to prevent him from turning toward him. For added pressure and discomfort, Camarillo points his knee toward Swick's sternum.

b. The pain and discomfort are so great, Swick is hardly focused on his outstretched right arm. Seizing this opportunity, Camarillo slides his right shin and hooked foot into Swick's armpit while continuously pulling up on his arm.

c. Without stopping, Camarillo lowers his level and thrusts his hips toward Swick's armpit. Without his hips in place, the armlock would be too loose and Swick could easily escape.

d. Camarillo steps his left foot in front of Swick's right shoulder and pinches his knees together as he falls to his back in a leg-side armbar.

e. In the finishing position, Camarillo's shins are now a wall that Swick cannot surpass or roll over. This makes it easy for Camarillo to squeeze his knees together and bridge his hips upward to hyperextend the elbow.

AFTER-ACTION REPORT:

For the knee-on-belly near-side armbar, the guerrilla easily moves to the arm by utilizing a sagging knee pressure to the solar plexus to create both distraction away from the arm attack and an urgency for the opponent to give up his arm. Once the arm is under control, the guerrilla must focus his attention and energies toward getting his lower shin inserted into the armpit.

SITREP 4.21 - KNEE-ON-BELLY: SPINNING ARMBAR

Once the knee-on-belly pressure is mastered there will be very few opponents and training partners willing to lie flat on their backs and wait for the pain and suffocation. Instead, they will feverishly fight to get to their sides and push the guerrilla away from the control. This is the type of reaction on which the guerrilla thrives. For one, it tires the opponent out much faster than the guerrilla and second, it exposes the far-side arm for the spinning arm attack. To the guerrilla, every pressing defense equates to the same thing—the spinning armbar!

Plan of Attack:

a. SUBJECT CAMARILLO is pressuring forward in the knee-on-belly position while CONTACT SWICK, MICHAEL turns toward him to escape either to his guard or to go to his knees in an attempt at a reversal. Camarillo has lowered his base and level to keep more weight on Swick, stifling his progress toward the escape.

b. Swick pushes away at Camarillo's hips with both hands as he tries to roll toward Camarillo. To counter, Camarillo places his hand on Swick's neck and hip to keep him on his back.

c. Mobility favors Camarillo and he is able to step over Swick's head easily and clamp down on his outstretched left arm by locking it under his armpit. While traversing to the side, Camarillo makes sure to grab the leg to set up the leg-side armbar.

d. Camarillo slides his left leg onto Swick's torso, locking Swick's arm between his legs. Before he falls to his back, Camarillo ensures he has a tight clamp on Swick's left arm by pressing his right elbow tight to his hip.

e. Due to the tight arm clamp, Camarillo just has to fall to his back to execute an incredibly tight armbar. Swick must tap immediately as the pressure on his elbow is overwhelming.

SNAFU MOMENT:

If the guerrilla fails to keep pressure on his opponent, he will likely have to deal with a single-leg attempt as he tries to circle his opponent's head. Pressure and hand-and-body placement are everything for controlling the top position. In the case that the opponent does make it to his knees, the guerrilla can always execute submissions off the single-leg, as in SITREPs 4.18 and 4.19.

AFTER-ACTION REPORT:

By mastering the pressure and positioning of SITREP 4.20, the guerrilla creates a fear and urgency to escape, and that is the type of reaction that leads to mistakes for the opponent. Any good guerrilla should be able to capitalize on these mistakes, and outstretched arms against the knee-on-belly should make any guerrilla salivate! As with many arm attacks, the key is to capture the arm as soon as it begins to push and then commit to the turn and finish. As with the spinning armbar from side control and the near-side knee-on-belly armbar, the guerrilla should focus on getting his shin flush to the armpit for a tight finishing position.

HUNTING ARMBARS FROM THE MOUNT

- Use the chest and torso to keep the arm isolated while mounted.
- Once the arm is crossed, never let your opponent pull his elbow back toward the floor.
- Chokes not only distract but must also be addressed. Use your opponent's choke defense to set up arm locks on his exposed arms. Just be sure to make the choke a viable threat!
- Learn to use your entire body and the mat to isolate a stubborn arm, but focus on the elbows.
- By S-mounting a leg in the mount, the guerrilla will be able to "lighten" his swinging leg. This allows the guerrilla to remove the weight from his leg and swing effortlessly and unimpeded.
- Always practice the basic self-defense armbar drill for speed and precision.

SITREP 4.22 - MOUNT: CROSLEY ARMBAR

Instead of jumping straight into armbar attacks from the mount, the guerrilla should first learn how to get to his Fire Team as he mounts. For SITREP 4.22, the guerrilla carries his momentum from the mount through to the finish. By practicing this way, the guerrilla learns to overwhelm his opponent through continuous motion. In this regard, the guerrilla must always remember that if he stops to collect himself, he allows his opponent the same luxury.

Assembling a Fire Team

SUBMIT EVERYONE

Plan of Attack:

a. From the side control position, SUBJECT CAMARILLO has switched his base so that his hips are facing CONTACT DARCY, MATTHEW. Camarillo has reached his left arm in front of Darcy's right knee and is pulling both his knees together as both a distraction and pinning technique. By keeping his right arm over Darcy's shoulder, he is also blocking Darcy's view of the action.

b. While Darcy is focused on his knees, Camarillo has all the time he needs: an instant. He snaps his left foot over Darcy's legs, locking his heel to Darcy's hip. Camarillo maintains a tight pinch with his right knee to prevent Darcy from trying to escape out the backdoor.

c. Immediately, Camarillo drops his left knee to the floor and then swims his left arm underneath Darcy's elbow. Camarillo also removes his right hand's shoulder grip and scoots both his feet underneath Darcy's knees to solidify the mounted position.

d. Camarillo forms a cross-face control with his right arm in front of Darcy's face and links both his hands together under Darcy's head. Now, Camarillo starts to pull his body toward Darcy's head, forcing Darcy's elbow up to his ear.

e. With Darcy's right elbow open, Camarillo can slide his left knee underneath it to both set up the armbar and prevent Darcy from returning his elbow to safety. Camarillo is careful to keep his weight equalized to avoid being rolled to his left side.

f. Camarillo shifts to an upright posture, slides his right foot under Darcy's left shoulder to form an "S-mount" control, and secures Darcy's right wrist as he gets closer to the finish.

g. Next Camarillo places his right hand on the floor for base and to block Darcy's hips as he goes for the leg-side armbar. Camarillo shifts his weight toward Darcy's legs to lighten his left leg and to make it much easier to swing in front of Darcy's face. Still, Camarillo will keep his head forward to keep weight over Darcy until the finish.

h. Camarillo completes swinging his leg over Darcy's face and finishes the leg-side armbar while hugging Darcy's right leg. With this leg control, Darcy is unable to sit toward Camarillo to defend the technique and will be forced to tap as his elbow hyperextends.

AFTER-ACTION REPORT:

Both guerrilla jiu-jitsu and attack-centered grappling rely on seizing opportunity for success. Though the movement does not necessarily have to be lightning-fast, continuous motion, especially when assisted by pressure and confidence in action, leads to immediate submission. If the guerrilla can get away with avoiding his opponent's defense by moving straight through him, he should. This is why all guerrillas must first practice their mounted fire team from the transition into mount to the finish. Later, they can add the guard pass and possibly the guard pull and sweep.

SITREP 4.23 - MOUNT: SD ARMBAR

The SD armbar is one of the most important drills for learning to recognize contact and act intuitively. In other words, this builds speed and lots of it! Though many may disregard the self-defense-style armbar as something that should last be practiced at white belt, they are wrong. There are plenty of moments when an opponent will momentarily push from any position and the guerrilla must be able to react instantly. Furthermore, the body mechanics learned through drilling are invaluable to other armbars from the top position.

Plan of Attack:

a.   SUBJECT CAMARILLO is again attacking from the mount position against CONTACT DARCY, MATTHEW. This time Camarillo has already achieved the mounted position and has pulled himself to an upright mount.

b. As Camarillo drives his weight into Darcy's chest, Darcy reacts by pushing into Camarillo's chest to escape and alleviate the pressure. Camarillo responds by keeping his hand posted on the chest, switching to an S-mount with his right foot and sliding his pelvis beneath Darcy's right armpit.

c. While shifting his weight toward Darcy's legs to allow his left leg to sweep easily over Darcy's face, Camarillo also must keep his chest forward to prevent Darcy from shucking his elbow downward to escape. The chest pressure is integral to keeping the arm locked forward.

d. Camarillo swipes his left leg over Darcy's face and is already bridging his hips forward to put pain on Darcy's right elbow. At this point, many will tap from the forward-pressing armbar.

e. With the arm already outstretched, Camarillo only has to fall back and the armbar is already on tight. Darcy is forced to tap from elbow hyperextension.

AFTER-ACTION REPORT:

The SD armbar is a staple for mounted attacks for any guerrilla. Though this movement is often used as a drill to develop fluid movement, timing, and speed, it is also practical on many levels. When dealing with pressure many opponents still push to resist or to find the space to get their arms to a better positioning. This is the time to attack.

For self-defense and MMA, strikes from the mount can be so devastating that fighters will do whatever it takes to escape, including pushing their opponent away in the hope of alleviating the strikes. Again, the guerrilla must be able to move decisively to take advantage of the exposed arms.

Regardless of the situation, this movement is key to feeling how to rapidly move the body from a parallel to a perpendicular attack angle from the mount. For new guerrillas, it is essential to practice this movement until it is second nature.

SITREP 4.24 - MOUNT: NINO ARMBAR FINISH

The Nino armbar finish is a move that first gained popularity with the jiu-jitsu whiz, Antonio "Nino" Schembri, but it has evolved into being more of a primary armbar for guerrillas. By attacking the armbar while still mounted, the guerrilla allows himself a primary arm attack with a great parachute. If the armbar fails, the guerrilla can resume the mount and start a new attack, whereas the traditional armbar may lead to the guard if the opponent manages to escape. This is important for non-armbar fire teams as well.

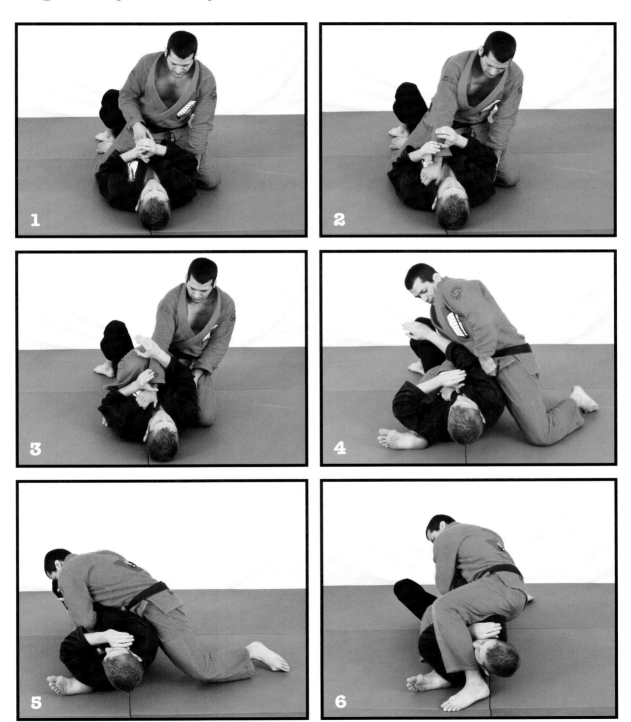

Plan of Attack:

a. As with the preceding SITREP, SUBJECT CAMARILLO begins in the upright or high mount against CONTACT DARCY, MATTHEW. This time, Camarillo grips Darcy's left lapel with his right hand and secures Darcy's right triceps. Camarillo uses a push on the lapel and pull on the arm to keep Darcy locked to the mat while exposing his arm for attack.

b. While consistently pulling the arm and pushing against his body, Camarillo baseball slides his right leg underneath Darcy's left arm for the "S-mount" while bringing his pelvis under Darcy's right armpit. Camarillo always moves his body to the arm the second it is exposed.

c. To secure the arm, Camarillo hugs Darcy's forearm with his left arm while his right hand posts on the mat to the right of Darcy's legs. Once more, Camarillo shifts his body toward Darcy's legs.

d. This time, Camarillo is ready to finish on top. He steps over Darcy's head and immediately bridges his hips upward into the elbow. Camarillo uses his hand on the mat to keep balance.

e. From this angle, it is clear that Camarillo must rely on his right hand to keep from falling back as his hips drive forward. Darcy cannot bring his right shoulder back to the mat to defend the position and is forced to submit.

SNAFU MOMENT—COMPROMISED BALANCE:

In a case where the guerrilla either falls forward or rearward while attempting the finish, he can move to a "facedown" juji gatame (juji roll series) or a standard leg-side armbar. With both options so obvious, the forward armbar should become a first line of attack option because its failure usually leads to the same end.

AFTER-ACTION REPORT:

All guerrillas must think and rethink their primary attacks from any top position. Does their fire team attack leave them overly exposed to reversals? Will the guerrilla end in the guard if the opponent escapes?

For the guerrilla attacker, these questions are important. The guerrilla should have in his repertoire at least one primary fire team attack that leaves him in the same position in case the attack goes FUBAR. Again, this is part of preparation, and through the preparation for failure, the guerrilla prepares for success.

Assembling a Fire Team

HUNTING THE ARMBAR FROM THE BACK

- Armbar attacks against the turtle have a tendency to catch many jiu-jitsu practitioners off-guard, though many judokas are prepared for them.
- Use the kimura as a block to prevent your opponent from turning toward the attack.
- Most expect chokes from the back over armbars. Use the same concepts of the mount by attacking the choke to free up the arms for attack.
- A belt-line hook is better for going into the arm attack from the back than a standard hook in front of the inner thigh.
- As with all armbars, it is critical that the guerrilla move his hips and pelvis to the armpit instead of hoping that the armpit will move to him.
- Try to push your opponent into an SAP for the best chance of securing the armlock without being pushed into the guard.

SITREP 4.25 - TURTLE: ARMBAR WHEN OPPONENT REACHES

The threat of having the back taken is strong for the opponent, and many advanced jiu-jitsu practitioners will do whatever it takes to prevent the hooks from being placed and losing the four points for the position. The guerrilla takes advantage of this logic in SITREP 4.25 as he attacks the arm that is trying to prevent the hooks. The guerrilla must always be up-to-date on the rules and methods of all grappling arts in order to exploit their weaknesses with his fire team.

Plan of Attack:

a. SUBJECT CAMARILLO has reached the top turtle position against CONTACT DARCY, MATTHEW. Camarillo is controlling Darcy's hips with both hands and Darcy is stiff-arming Camarillo's left knee to prevent him from using his hooks (feet) to take the back.

b. Unbeknownst to Darcy, he has just overexposed his left arm. Camarillo immediately wraps his right hand over the top of Darcy's arm to secure it while his left hand posts to the mat. Throughout the action, Camarillo jumps his right shin across Darcy's upper back.

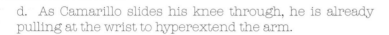

c. Camarillo slides his right shin clear across the back of Darcy's neck while he posts on his forehead and hand to keep his balance. Camarillo does not wish to get bullied into the guard position.

d. As Camarillo slides his knee through, he is already pulling at the wrist to hyperextend the arm.

e. To finish the hold, Camarillo points his knee upward and locks his left leg over Darcy's arm. Camarillo ensures that the thumb is pointed away from the opposing angle of hyperextension and finishes Darcy with the armbar.

AFTER-ACTION REPORT:

As with all guerrilla attacks, knowledge leads to preparation, and the guerrilla arms himself with the commonality that jiu-jitsu players defend the hooks at all costs! Unfortunately for opponents, the guerrilla is not only concerned with getting points; he is more focused on exposure and the finish. If the opponent does not defend his back this way, the guerrilla can continue to move forward to take the hooks and then move once more to his preferred fire team attack.

SITREP 4.24 - BACK: ARMBAR FROM THE BACK

The armbar from the back is far less common than the rear-naked choke and lapel choke, but what it does do, it does well! When fighting an opponent whose grip-fighting and choke defense is strong, this is often the best route to get to the finish. Using the kimura for body control, the guerrilla is able to move the fight to a favorable submission and out of a stalemate. This also creates the added psychological advantage of disrupting the opponent mentally as he is unprepared for such a change in position and defense.

Assembling a Fire Team

Plan of Attack:

a. SUBJECT CAMARILLO has taken the back of CONTACT DARCY, MATTHEW. Camarillo has an over-and-under control and both he and Darcy are facing upward. At this point, Darcy is more concerned with a possible choke and is defending by pulling down on Camarillo's right sleeve.

b. As Darcy focuses on defending a possible choke, Camarillo weaves his left hand in front of him and then grips Darcy's left wrist while he "gas-pedals" Darcy's right hip with his right foot. Even though he is changing position, Camarillo maintains the threat of the choke to keep Darcy in defense.

c. Camarillo falls to his left side and makes sure to keep his head inside of Darcy's left ear. This blocks Darcy from getting his shoulders to the mat to escape on Camarillo's left side. Again, Camarillo continues the feint by attacking the choke as he slides his left leg across Darcy's lower abdomen in a belt-line hook.

d. Closing in on the final position, Camarillo reaches over Darcy's left shoulder with his right hand and exchanges his forearm grip with his left hand and then finishes the figure-four lock by gripping his right wrist with his left hand. Next, Camarillo pushes down with his right foot on the "gas pedal" or hip. This shifts Darcy downward while allowing Camarillo to move his hips toward Darcy's left shoulder.

e. Camarillo punches the figure-four grip into Darcy to force him onto his back. As he does so, he steps his right leg over his head to get to the head-side SAP.

f. Focusing on the forearm, Camarillo sits forward, twists the kimura lock toward his head to break Darcy's grip and begins falling back.

g. Camarillo finishes the submission by arching his hips upward to hyperextend Darcy's left elbow. Darcy is forced to tap to the submission or face ligament damage.

SNAFU MOMENT—FORGETTING THE BELT-LINE HOOK:

The belt-line hook not only makes it easier for the guerrilla to move to the armbar, it also helps prevent a possible counter. If the guerrilla keeps his hooks in the standard position, there is a possibility that a savvy opponent will lock the leg in a half guard and try to roll toward the guerrilla to counter with pressure and possibly pass the guard.

AFTER-ACTION REPORT:

Although the guerrilla should often practice the whole movement of taking the back from the turtle through to the finish, as seen in the following movement (SITREP 4.25), it is valuable for the guerrilla to first learn how to use the kimura lock and hip movement against the standard back attack to get acquainted with the submission's complexities.

Beyond entries, this movement is excellent against opponents with strong collar and choke defense because their arms are so available for attack.

SITREP 4.25 - BACK: TURTLE TO BACK ARMBAR

Whereas SITREP 4.24 focuses on the finish from the standard back control with hooks, SITREP 4.25 takes it up a notch by attacking from the turtle to the back to the finish. Again, constant motion and staying focused on the finish lead to domination for the guerrilla and a feeling of futility for the opponent, who is overwhelmed by the attack. It cannot be stated enough how important it is to always fight for the finish without stopping to develop an aggressive, attack-oriented game.

Assembling a Fire Team

SUBMIT EVERYONE

Plan of Attack:

a. SUBJECT CAMARILLO begins with his left hand establishing a tight control of the right lapel of CONTACT DARCY, MATTHEW . Camarillo grips toward his body for greater body control while clamping down with his left elbow on Darcy's left flank to prevent a possible reversal.

b. Moving to the technical phase, Darcy is in the turtle position with Camarillo on top. Utilizing the previous details, Camarillo has the cross-lapel control with his left elbow free and is keeping his weight behind Darcy's hips to avoid being rolled. Darcy's hands are defensive.

c. Darcy feels unmovable, so Camarillo kicks his right leg upward behind him to create momentum. Meanwhile, Camarillo maintains connection with the mat with his left foot in case he has to change directions or restabilize the position.

d. Sharply, Camarillo kicks his right knee downward and into Darcy's right knee. This topples Darcy's right knee inward and allows Camarillo to pull Darcy onto his lap with his left hand.

e. Camarillo continues to pull Darcy onto his lap until they are both facing upward. At this point, Camarillo extends his right hook underneath Darcy's right calf muscle to extend his leg while he inserts his left hook. Camarillo releases his grip on the lapel in preparation for the figure-four lock. He will grip Darcy's left wrist with his right hand to lock the figure-four lock.

f. As with the previous SITREP, Camarillo locks the figure-four lock and falls to his left side. Already, he starts to push the grip into Darcy to move him back toward the floor.

g. Camarillo swings his leg over Darcy's face aggressively. Searching for a defendable position, Darcy desperately clasps his hands together to buy himself some time.

h. Camarillo sits up with Darcy, pulls his elbow to his chest, and begins torquing the kimura. With this pressure alone, Darcy's defense is already being pushed to the limit.

i. The grip breaks and Darcy has nothing else to grip. He tries to roll out, but Camarillo has clamped down over his head and body and is mindful to keep Darcy's thumb pointed skyward for control.

j. All that Camarillo needs to do is fall back into the submission and, of course, that is exactly what he does. Camarillo submits Darcy by hyperextending his left elbow.

SNAFU MOMENT—ELBOW AWARENESS:

A guerrilla never allows his opponent to grip or control his elbows while he is on top of the turtle position. This can lead to rolling reversals or kimura submissions. Instead, the guerrilla uses his opponent's lapels to maintain superior hip control or body lock grips with his elbows to the outside to control his opponent's hips.

AFTER-ACTION REPORT:

This movement has it all: momentum and velocity in taking the back, direct action in getting immediately to the kimura instead of going traditional to take the back hooks, and the kimura-to-armbar finish, which can be attacked from so many other positions. In the same vein as the mounted armbar that is initiated by first taking the mount, SITREP 4.25 never allows the opponent to feel comfortable; he simply is not allowed the time to move into his defensive posture. Once more, this ideal should be pursued in every element of jiu-jitsu. Whether it is of a defensive or offensive origin, the goal is to get to the finish and win!

SECTION TWO: Submissions Against Any Opponent

Although a martial artist does not welcome or invite conflict into his life, he must be prepared to fight anyone, regardless of stature. This is why choosing a fire team is so important.

The guerrilla's fire team attack must be capable of attacking and submitting a heavier, stronger, faster, more flexible, and more explosive opponent. This is the essence of martial arts, and it takes complete dedication for a guerrilla to make one attack work against the vast majority of opponents. However, when the attack does work against the strong and athletic, it will be even easier against opponents of similar size.

For the guerrilla to develop his fire team, he should focus on control points that stifle movement and range, and deflect power. They are there in every technique waiting for the guerrilla to discover them.

This is why SUBJECT CAMARILLO focuses on the armlock against the big and strong as well as the small and flexible. Often enough, a bully passer tries to bulldoze past his guard or bench press to escape, and Camarillo can use his speed and experience to achieve a lightning-fast lock. For the small and flexible, he can ramp up the control for a slow and deliberate anaconda-like submission. In either case, he believes in his fire team and is prepared for success.

SECTION THREE: Combinations that Make Sense

The fire team cannot rely solely on direct attack for success, but also must use other tools as well. This section, will focus on the use of combinations to get to the fire team finish. While creating their combinations, it is vital that guerrillas use strong secondary attack entries, simplicity, and flow.

Developing secondary submission entries is critical if the guerrilla hopes to get to his preferred fire team. These submissions are secondary in nature, and the guerrilla may not be at the same level of proficiency with them in terms of finishing as the primary fire team finish, but he should have a high level of proficiency in the entry phase. After all, this is the most important phase when it comes to creating a combination that feeds off the opponent's defensive movement or evasiveness.

Keep It Simple Stupid or KISS should be the golden rule for all guerrillas at all times, but especially when creating and evolving their preferred combinations. The fancier or more intricate the combination, the less likely it will be successful when it comes time to execute the attack plan. The guerrilla must recall that if it takes twenty-five movements to execute one attack, that is twenty-five opportunities for an opponent to insert his escape. Keep it simple!

When it comes to creating flow in the attack series, the guerrilla may wish to consult chapter 2, section 2's basic combinations to ensure that the movements logically flow into and out of each other. There is no utility in completely unrelated attacks that are too difficult to segue between!

So, to recap, the guerrilla must focus on secondary entries to get to primary attacks, make sure these are simple and repeatable, and that they logically flow with each other.

SITREP 4.26 - OMOPLATA ROLL WITH SPINNING ARMBAR

SUBJECT CAMARILLO loves the juji gatame armbar because it easily fits in with any other submission. SITREP 4.26 is a great showcase of how the armbar works with the omoplata, especially when the opponent either rolls to escape or is swept to his back using the attack. All the guerrilla has to do is simply follow his opponent's POE and he automatically arrives in an easily attackable position for his preferred fire team. Again, this takes advantage of a strong secondary attack in the omoplata entry with a simple transition that flows directly to an easy submission.

Plan of Attack:

a. SUBJECT CAMARILLO has reached the omoplata shoulder lock against CONTACT THOMSON, JOSHUA. Camarillo has an upright posture and is hugging Thomson's lower back to inhibit an easy forward roll escape by Thomson.

b. Rolling is too difficult an option for Thomson. Instead, he begins to push off the floor with his right hand and walks his hips toward Camarillo. While executing this movement, Thomson is focused on keeping his hips high to prevent Camarillo from breaking his hip down to the mat. If that happens, it's over for him and he knows it.

c. Driving off the floor with his right hand and legs, Thomson jumps his body into Camarillo in attempt to scramble free from the position. Instead of fighting the action, Camarillo flows with the momentum and goes facedown while extending his legs.

d. By going facedown, Camarillo allows Thomson to pass safely over the top of him to his back. At this point, Camarillo clamps down on Thomson's left arm, making sure it does not budge from underneath his right armpit. This will prevent Thomson from turning toward him to escape to a positive position.

e. Pushing off the mat with his right hand to propel himself on top of Thomson, Camarillo also circles his left leg counter-clockwise until his left leg crosses Thomson's face. Throughout, Camarillo makes certain that Thomson does not escape his left arm.

f. From the "cowboy" or saddle mount, Camarillo slides his rear to the mat so his pelvis is sucked close to Thomson's left armpit. Camarillo's right hand is on the mat, clamping down on Thomson's left arm.

g. Camarillo crosses his right leg over Thomson's head and hugs his near-side leg to prevent him from sitting forward to escape. To finish the leg-side armbar, Camarillo hugs the outside of his head-side quadriceps, pinches his knees together, bridges his hips upward, and finishes with the elbow extension.

AFTER-ACTION REPORT:

The omoplata, especially the rolling escape or sweep, directly leads to the armbar because the omoplata already does so much work for the armbar. By isolating the opponent's arm with his legs and hip, the guerrilla has to do very little except follow the POE (path of escape) to arrive in the easy-to-finish position. As long as he stays glued to that arm and he puts his focus on moving with the arm more than the body, the guerrilla should be able to successfully finish off the roll.

When developing this submission combination, the guerrilla should first focus on speed and control in getting to the omoplata and then breaking the posture to force the roll. The rest is hanging on for the ride to the submission!

SITREP 4.27 - ELBOW PULL TO TRIANGLE ARMBAR

For SITREP 4.27, the guerrilla uses KISS to play with action and reaction to get to his fire team. By attacking the arm in a standard armbar, the guerrilla is able to take advantage of a strong pulling resistance to set up his much easier triangle entry. From here, it is far too easy for the guerrilla to flow into the closely related triangle armbar. Nowhere in this scenario does the guerrilla try to reinvent the wheel; instead he focuses on simplicity and economy of movement to get to the fire team finish.

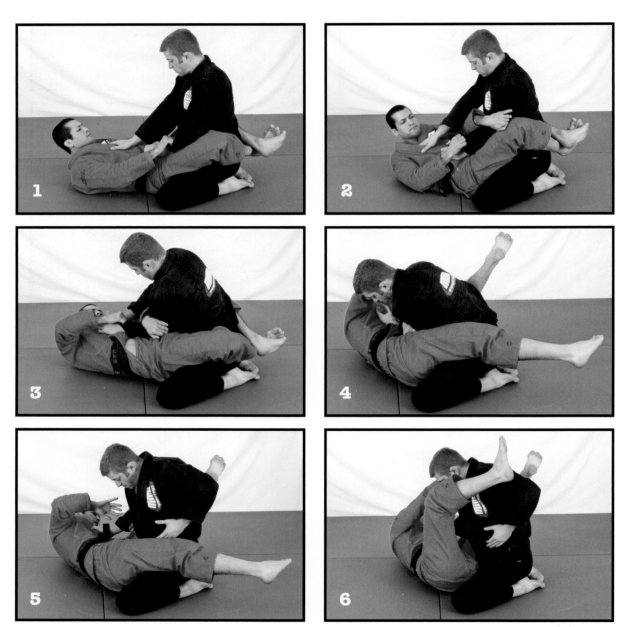

Plan of Attack:

a. SUBJECT CAMARILLO begins on the bottom of closed guard with CONTACT DARCY, MATTHEW, on top and in posture. Darcy has a staggered arm posture to prevent himself from being easily pulled downward while also limiting Camarillo's ability to sit forward or lift his hips. Camarillo controls with a same-sided hooked grip against Darcy's rear sleeve.

b. Camarillo swims his left hand underneath Darcy's forward arm and grips behind Darcy's left elbow. This creates a "backstop" that limits Darcy's ability to pull his elbow backward to escape the armlock or control. Camarillo will attack this rear arm as a ploy to isolate Darcy's forward arm.

c. The trap is ready. Camarillo opens his legs and points his toes to the left to move his hips out to the right. This forces Darcy to address the very real threat of the armbar on his left arm, and he reacts by hunching down and powering his left arm backward against the backstop.

d. As Camarillo feels Darcy struggling to escape his elbow, he releases the backstop and grips Darcy's right lapel with his right hand. As Darcy's arm escapes the armbar, his forward right arm is now exposed for the triangle. Camarillo pulls with the lapel and lunges his legs upward to lock the triangle.

e. The early triangle is locked, and Camarillo continues to control Darcy's lapel with his right hand and Darcy's sleeve with his left.

f. To alter the angle, Camarillo switches his left hand to his shin as his right hand hugs Darcy's wrist. With his shin and arm making a triangle, Camarillo can put his foot on Darcy's hip and escape his hips to the right for a better angle.

g. Instead of returning to the triangle or trying to alter the angle of the choke, Camarillo opts for the fast finish. He slaps his left leg in front of Darcy's face, hugs Darcy's wrist with both arms, and explosively lifts his hips upward to hyperextend the elbow.

SNAFU MOMENT-DEFENDING THE UNDERHOOK PASS:

With one arm under the leg, the single-underhook pass is always a threat. For the guerrilla a fast explosive hip movement can defeat the opponent before he has the time to walk around the guard. The opponent cannot pass the guard if he is unable to use a stacking pressure. A good guerrilla keeps a strong pull on the arm and is always ready to attack with the triangle if necessary.

AFTER-ACTION REPORT:

If the guerrilla was to spring the triangle without creating the desired pulling reaction in the opponent, he would be far less successful in his attack and might possibly set up a counter. By leading the opponent to resist, the guerrilla can apply a secondary submission entry that he may not even be the greatest at! Guerrillas should remember the importance of setting up their entries to make the combinations and finishes much easier down the road.

SECTION FOUR: Submissions against the Defense

While it is of obvious importance to have a fire team that works in any position, against any type of opponent, and with great combinations, all of this is worth far less if the guerrilla cannot overcome the simple defenses to the fire team itself. In this section, we will show how the guerrilla beats the fire team defenses. This is the final element to mastery of a fire team submission.

When creating an attack-through-defenses game plan, the guerrilla should think about a few essential elements for greater achievement. First, he should always reevaluate his attack and finishing positioning. Is he using his weight, grips, body, and positioning correctly? This must be fixed prior to moving forward. Second, he must analyze the defensive grips that are preventing the finish. Oftentimes, a simple grip break is the only thing the guerrilla needs to accomplish for the finish. Third, the guerrilla should make sure he disrupts the opponent's base or platform of defense. If this platform becomes unstable, so does his ability to efficiently defend the fire team assault. Finally, the guerrilla must be able to combine all these elements to assist him in changing the angle of attack. By changing the angle, the guerrilla affords himself the ability to go around the opponent's defense.

Knowledge of defensive tactics is invaluable and it is suggested that all good guerrilla attackers spend time playing with their defense to better understand what they need to do to escape the submission. Then, by parlaying this knowledge to the attack, the guerrilla is better suited to devising his own counterstrategy.

SITREP 4.30 - STACKED ELBOW OPENING

Every submission hunter must learn to deal with the stack or forward pressure. This can be exhausting for the bottom grappler as his diaphragm is compressed and breathing becomes more difficult. For SITREP 4.30, the guerrilla distracts and off-balances his opponent's defense by disrupting his base and then removes the defensive grip to reexpose the arm for the attack. As soon as the arm comes free, the guerrilla immediately goes into his fire team end game. Once more, simple tactics lead to victory.

Plan of Attack:

a. SUBJECT CAMARILLO is attacking the armbar from the closed guard against CONTACT DARCY, MATTHEW. Darcy is defending by locking his left arm over his right hand at the elbow to prevent it from being stretched out.

b. Always thinking of attacking the periphery and off-balancing, Camarillo pushes Darcy's left knee open to destabilize his defensive positioning.

c. While Darcy tries to regain his balance, Camarillo brings his right palm underneath Darcy's elbow and presses it upward. This overwhelms Darcy, as he now has to focus on two things at once: his disrupted equilibrium and hiding his right arm from attack.

d. Success! Camarillo punches Darcy's elbow upward and away from the arm it was protecting. Already, Camarillo is driving down on Darcy's head with his left leg as he pounces on the arm.

e. Without any way to defend the arm, Camarillo bridges his hips upward and finishes the armbar attack. Again, Darcy is forced to submit from a hyperextended right elbow.

SNAFU MOMENT—PUSHING AND PULLING:

Not realizing where to push and pull in the closed guard armbar is a critical mistake. The guerrilla must understand that his legs need to keep his opponent away from a stacking pressure while his hips and arm lock the arm to his own body. Keeping with this simple idea means success for any attacker.

AFTER-ACTION REPORT:

By pushing on the opponent's knee, the guerrilla is able to destabilize the defensive opponent. This has the added benefit of forcing the defender to reset his stacking posture. As he moves to reset, the guerrilla pops the arm free and finishes the attack. Through distraction and off-balancing, the guerrilla is able to finally finish his original mission—to successfully hit the fire team submission.

For guerrillas with other fire team submissions, this first lesson is still the most important. Do not give up on the submission and retreat at the first sign of defense. If the submission has the support of good positioning and a strong entry, the guerrilla should be able to continue by focusing on eliminating the obstacles on the way to the tap.

SITREP 4.31 - STACKED ARMBAR OVER DEFENSE

SITREP 4.31 is the first sign of building an end game as the opponent moves to defend the grip-break of SITREP 4.30. When the opponent bears down on the arm to prevent the arm under attack from being pulled through, he actually exposes the arm on the other side. The guerrilla only has to change from pushing the elbow away from the body to pushing it toward the body for exposure! This is a sneaky attack that illustrates how deep you can go while creating a grip-breaking game plan for your preferred fire team.

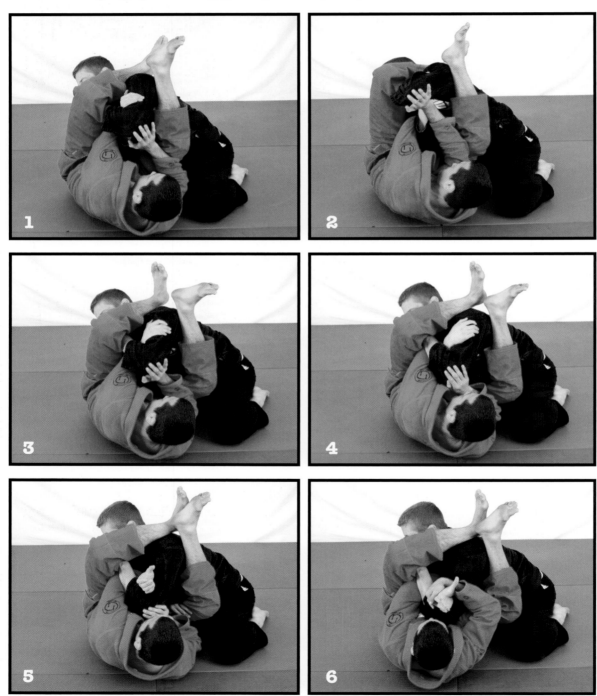

Plan of Attack:

a. SUBJECT CAMARILLO is attacking the armbar from the closed guard against CONTACT DARCY, MATTHEW. Darcy is defending by locking his left arm over his right hand at the elbow to prevent it from being stretched out. As with the previous SITREP, Camarillo is attempting to push Darcy's left elbow high enough to expose his arm for the submission.

b. Camarillo presses hard to expose enough of Darcy's wrist to pull it through for the submission. Though startled, Darcy is resisting by powering his elbow back toward the protected arm.

c. As Camarillo feels Darcy resisting the elbow exposure by pressing his left elbow downward, he opts to go with the momentum. Instead of resisting, Camarillo switches to pushing in at the elbow with his right hand. When combined with Darcy's momentum, Camarillo easily pushes the elbow deep enough to expose much of Darcy's right wrist.

d. With Darcy's right wrist exposed, Camarillo reaches over the top and begins pulling down to continue with the tight armbar attack. Darcy's left arm is no longer a factor; in fact, at the angle it is under the arm, it will only serve as another fulcrum to lever the arm for the lock.

c. Camarillo secures Darcy's arm with both hands, arches his hips upward, and hyperextends Darcy's right elbow. Darcy is forced to submit from the pain or risk ligament damage. His arm is far too trapped to be an effective defense.

AFTER-ACTION REPORT:

Feeling when to change gears in an attack is important when creating a strong attacking style. In this case, the opponent drives his elbow tight to his body to prevent his assisting arm from being pushed away from the arm under protection. The guerrilla must feel this and then redirect his counter to go with this motion, pushing the arm even further toward the body to expose the wrist and minimize the effectiveness of blocking the submission.

SITREP 4.32 - PENDULUM TO ARMBAR

Balance is everything in grappling, and guerrillas like to see their opponents balanced as if they are on the head of a pin. When it comes to beating the defensive posture of the armbar from the guard, the guerrilla also understands that his opponent has little base to his front corner if he is rocked in that direction. Therefore, the guerrilla will work tirelessly to angle his body so that he can rock his opponent to that corner. This sets up a dilemma for the defender—get rocked to his back for the sweep or post an arm and deal with the arm attack.

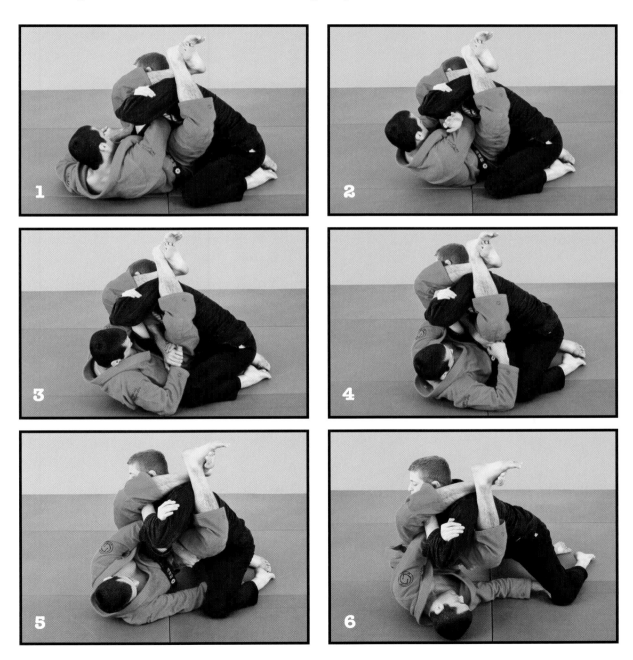

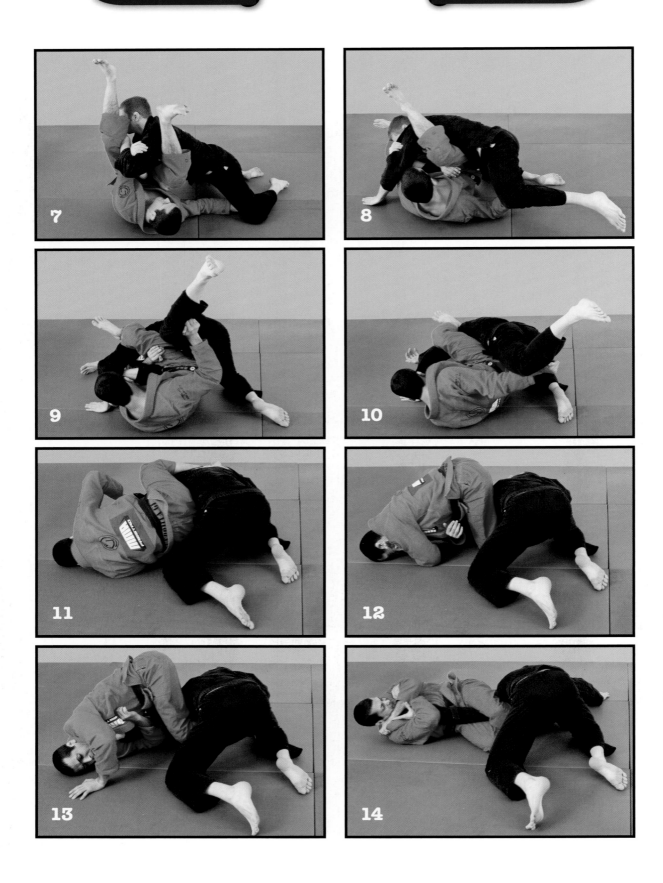

SUBMIT EVERYONE

Plan of Attack:

a. SUBJECT CAMARILLO has reached the armbar from the closed guard position against CONTACT DARCY, MATTHEW. Darcy is defending by lacing his left arm over his right to prevent his right arm from being straightened. Camarillo's right arm is threaded through and elbow-to-elbow with Darcy's.

b. In the same fashion as the SAP grip exchange, Camarillo locks his hands together and pulls his right arm back. This feeds his left elbow into the same attack position without omitting grips in the exchange. Darcy maintains his defensive grip throughout.

c. Once more, Camarillo pushes Darcy's left leg away to destabilize his defensive positioning. Camarillo uses a strong stiff-arm to give the push greater impetus.

d. With Darcy's base opened, Camarillo now rocks his legs to the left while lifting with his right hand as Darcy tries to bring his legs closer to his body. This gives Darcy a sense that he will head face-first into the mat or be rolled over. He instinctively posts his left hand on the mat to brace himself.

e. With Darcy's body so far forward, his legs become far lighter. This heightens Camarillo's ability to easily lift Darcy's leg and keep him off balance.

f. Darcy is extremely off-balanced and his left arm is now exposed by being posted on the mat. Camarillo attacks. He circles his right arm counterclockwise over and around Darcy's left arm and his right shin slides behind Darcy's head to secure the facedown, or more accurately, hips-facing, armbar.

g. To finish, Camarillo rolls all the way through until he is facing Darcy's hips with his own right hip on the mat. The finish is the same elbow hyperextension and Darcy is forced to tap as Camarillo moves his shoulders back and thrusts his hips forward.

SNAFU MOMENT—FACE DOWN vs. HIPS-FACING:

All guerrillas should try to avoid the facedown armbar for two primary reasons: it does not allow total body movement in the bridging phase of the finish and it inadequately defends against the opponent's ability to jump over the body and into side control. By finishing on the side, the guerrilla can bridge his entire body without being blocked by the mat and can follow his opponent into the SAP if he tries the jumping escape.

AFTER-ACTION REPORT:

While addressing the defender, the guerrilla realizes that his opponent has no defense to his front corners, so he naturally rocks him in that direction. This is sound grappling, as it creates two bad options for the defensive grappler—post a hand to block the sweep and possibly be submitted or be swept to the back and be submitted from the SAP.

SITREP 4.33 - PENDULUM TO HIPS-FACING ARMBAR

Faced with the previous pendulum-style arm attack of SITREP 4.32, many opponents will tense their bodies and bear down into the stack to avoid being rolled. Though this makes the pendulum unlikely, it does create the opportunity for the guerrilla to invert into the opponent and come out the back door into the hips-facing armbar. In addition, this is great jiu-jitsu in that it follows the motion of the stacking pressure and will actually assist the opponent's motion until he is facedown in the armlock!

Plan of Attack:

a. SUBJECT CAMARILLO has attacked the armbar from the closed guard against CONTACT DARCY, MATTHEW. Darcy has defended the position with the standard arm-to-arm defensive lock, and Camarillo has already threaded his left arm into the attack while pushing at Darcy's left knee. Camarillo clamps his own thigh to create constant pressure against the primary armbar.

b. As Darcy tries to pressure forward to "stack" Camarillo, Camarillo counters by bridging his hips into Darcy. This drives Camarillo onto his right shoulder and opens a large space between Camarillo's torso and Darcy's lower body.

c. Next, Camarillo swims his right arm in front of Darcy's right leg. This will help Camarillo pull his body through to the other side and will prevent Darcy from blocking the rotation with his knee.

d. Camarillo tucks his head to the inside and must spin clockwise on his upper back as his right hand helps to push Darcy away to free his head from underneath.

e. As he finishes his spin, Camarillo ends on his side. This forces Darcy to fall head-first into the mat.

f. Camarillo finishes the hips-facing armbar by securing Darcy's wrist with both arms, binding his arm to his own upper body. The finish comes as Camarillo bridges his hips into Darcy's elbow joint while escaping his shoulders back to lever his wrist. Darcy is forced to submit from elbow hyperextension.

SNAFU MOMENT—FOLLOWING THE ROLL:

Some novice and introductory-level opponents will seek to scramble out of this submission by rolling forward. In this case, do not worry. Just follow them into the SAP position and finish with a basic cross-body juji gatame. In fact, this knowledge of basic body mechanics will only help the guerrilla before working on the following defensive counter into the famed juji roll.

AFTER-ACTION REPORT:

By inverting into his opponent, the guerrilla is able to diffuse the power of the stacking pressure and will actually redirect his opponent into a facedown position with his arm extended in the submission. This movement works great with SITREP 4.33 as a one-two punch combination.

For the finish, the guerrilla should stay on his side where he can follow any counter as discussed in the SNAFU moment. Do not go facedown if you wish to prevent the counter!

SITREP 4.34 - HIPS-FACING TO JUJI ROLL ARMBAR

SITREPs 4.34 to 4.36 deal with finishing from the hips-facing armbar against different defensive scenarios. The guerrilla must remember that although he is close to the finish, a gutsy or knowledgeable opponent will seek to counter the position all the way until the end. For SITREP 4.34, the counter involves a redirection that leaves the opponent on his back in the SAP and then submission.

Plan of Attack:

a. SUBJECT CAMARILLO has reached the hips-facing armbar against CONTACT DARCY, MATTHEW. This time, Darcy is clamping down ferociously on his right arm to prevent it from being straightened. Camarillo counters this by clasping the top of Darcy's right foot with his right hand.

b. Camarillo pulls the foot over his body. This torques Darcy's knee and forces him to allow the leg to pass over Camarillo. Also, by pulling at the foot, Camarillo works with maximum efficiency by pulling at the end of a lever.

c. As Camarillo pulls Darcy's leg clear across his body to his right side, Darcy begins to fall—he has no basing arm to catch his body. Throughout the rotation, Camarillo follows with his torso.

d. Darcy falls to the mat and is again in the SAP.

e. Camarillo turns toward Darcy's legs to pry the arm free of its defensive cradle.

f. With the arm exposed, Camarillo can fall backward into a fully committed cross-body juji gatame. Darcy is forced to submit from a hyperextended right elbow.

AFTER-ACTION REPORT:

The guerrilla is able to easily pull the defensive opponent from the hip-facing armbar to the SAP and finish because the opponent is unable to post an arm for balance as the guerrilla moves his legs from one side to the other. This is possible because the guerrilla is facing the hips and is working at an angle where he can follow the arm in a clockwise path. If he was lying facedown, the pull (though impossible) would simply move the opponent from an armbar position into a passing one.

Similar to the pendulum series of counters, the guerrilla always thinks of how the opponent can catch his balance with his arms. If he cannot catch his balance, it is time to use a reversal to get to a top-dominant position where weight can assist in the finishing action.

SITREP 4.35 - KUZUSHI FOR ALTERNATE SHOULDER ROLL

All of grappling is evolution, and that is why seasoned grapplers can be so difficult. In this case, the defender does not wish to be rolled to his back as in SITREP 4.34 and is defending by hiding his foot under his rear. Though this prevents the previous roll, it also compromises his base to the rear right corner. Again, the guerrilla must feel this hole in his defense so he can instantly move to a Granby-style shoulder change and shoulder roll of his own to rock the defender backward into the SAP and fire team finish.

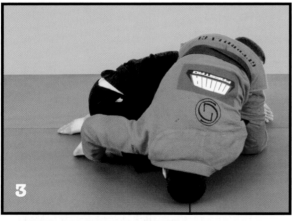

Plan of Attack:

a. SUBJECT CAMARILLO has attacked the hips-facing arm-bar against CONTACT DARCY, MATTHEW. Darcy has defended well by locking his left elbow over his right wrist to prevent his right arm from being straightened. In addition, Darcy is fighting with all his might to prevent Camarillo from pulling his right leg over his body for the juji roll finish.

b. As Camarillo feels Darcy bearing down with his right leg to defend, he counters again. This time, he follows Darcy's momentum by rolling on his shoulders and pushing Darcy's head upward with his left leg.

c. Camarillo continues to push and circle his body underneath until he is back in the armbar position from closed guard. Still, this is not the end point for Camarillo's countermotion.

d. By continuing to move with Darcy's original momentum, Camarillo has managed to push Darcy's back all the way to the mat.

e. Camarillo arrives in the leg-side SAP. From the onset of the technique to here, Camarillo has moved deliberately and without delay.

f. Camarillo finishes the leg-side armbar by falling toward the legs, both to pry the arm free and to prevent Darcy from sitting upright or turning toward him. Darcy is forced to submit from a hyperextended right elbow.

SNAFU MOMENT—MISSING MOMENTUM:

Guerrillas need to fight and skirmish to become successful, but they also need to be more like water. They have to find the holes in the rock and be flexible in their attacks to get to those holes. In this way, moving with the momentum of the fight can provide easy submissions and victories, especially when originating from a point of attack. A guerrilla learns to stay with the submission, but also to use momentum to get to the next point of attack.

AFTER-ACTION REPORT:

While defending SITREP 4.34 by hiding the "pulling" leg under the rear, the opponent leaves himself without adequate base to his rear corner. The guerrilla must adjust accordingly to be able to rock the opponent backward, and it is just as important that he learns to fluidly move from shoulder to shoulder to get to the proper side of the attack. This inverting motion should be ironed out and practiced regularly so the guerrilla can act instantly.

SITREP 4.36 - JUJI ROLL W/KNEE PICK

In this final defense against the hips-facing armbar, the opponent is staying tense, low, and strong while laying his body straight to prevent himself from being rocked backward and to make it difficult for his leg to be pulled over the guerrilla for the reversal. In this scenario, the guerrilla must do what he does best—stay with the attack. The opponent is extremely defensive, which means that with a little creativity, in this case the knee pick, the opponent will be on his back and submitting in no time.

Assembling a Fire Team

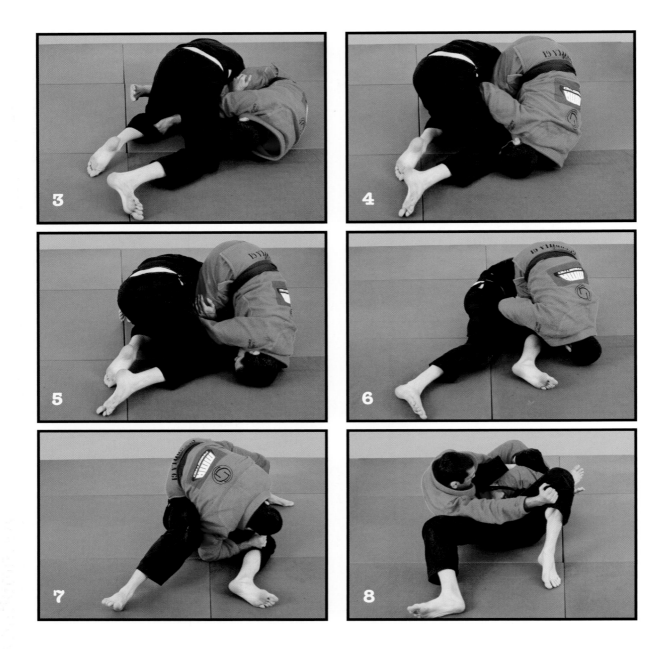

Plan of Attack:

a. SUBJECT CAMARILLO has reached the hips-facing armbar against CONTACT DARCY, MATTHEW. Darcy has defended the armbar by clamping his arm, defended the juji roll by keeping his right leg heavy to the mat, and defended the previous armbar by driving his head heavily to the mat. This signals to Camarillo to again change directions.

b. Camarillo cannot roll Darcy or push on his head, so he reaches his right arm in front of Darcy's right knee and grabs his left knee.

c. By pulling on the knee, Camarillo begins to topple Darcy to his left shoulder. Darcy cannot counter by posting his left hand. If he does so, he will forgo his defensive grip and be armbarred with a hips-facing armbar.

d. Darcy's posture is broken down all the way to his left hip. At this point, Camarillo thrusts his hips backward to ascend to the top position.

e. Camarillo continues to thrust his hips onto Darcy until he has reached the top position. He also continues to pull at the knee for balance and control.

f. Camarillo ends in the leg-side SAP and is ready to finish yet another armbar submission.

AFTER-ACTION REPORT:

By reaching under the opponent and pulling on his far knee, the attacker is able to off-balance his opponent's left and lower-left flank. When combined with a strong pushing motion from the hips (i.e., bridge), the guerrilla is able to take advantage of this with a simple pull of the pant leg and arm control and push of the hips to get into a top SAP.

For the guerrilla, this plan of attack is easy because the defender has committed his entire body to defending and left himself with no avenue for escape or evasion. Whenever a guerrilla finds himself in these waters, he should focus and continue because he is at a supreme advantage to finish the attack. His victim has locked himself away from the escape!

CONFIDENTIAL INFORMATION

Victory Belt

1209-83-68-888

FILE 005

Testing the Waters

FILE 005: TESTING THE WATERS

When it comes to testing the waters and learning what to attack and when to attack it, the guerrilla focuses on three elements: the direct attack, the indirect attack, and skill development. Only through complete understanding of all three will he become a master submission ace.

For submission artists, exposure is key and a direct or obvious attack is surely the best route to rapid success. However, creating an obvious attack is often more complicated than the attack itself, and that is where the indirect attack plays a part. By attacking something else, sometimes an obvious attack becomes available.

However, neither exists in a vacuum, and both elements must be supported by real-world physical ability. This is where skill development comes into play. Without the proper skill, all the technical knowledge and combination play is still just guesswork.

Bridging these three elements back to the subject matter at hand—how does a guerrilla know what to attack and when to attack it? He should attack the obvious item that is most exposed. This should be attacked when it has been adequately made available (often through indirect attack) and it should be attacked immediately and without delay.

SECTION ONE: The Direct Attack

The direct or obvious attack is the one that every defensive opponent sees coming, but fails to adequately prevent. It is the outstretched arm, the unprotected neck, and the dangling foot. It is essentially the free meal for the guerrilla submission artist.

Creating the obvious attack is something different altogether. The two primary avenues to the obvious attack are posture and grip breaking combined with deflection for the guard player to expose the arm or neck and secondary attacks or transitions to expose a defensive arm for the top player.

In both situations, the next step is simple, initiate a direct attack that best takes advantage of the vulnerable target and attack it with extreme focus to ensure total success.

SITREP 5.0 - CREATING AN OBVIOUS ARM ATTACK

In the example of SITREP 5.0, SUBJECT CAMARILLO is using a combination of hand deflection with a hip-thrust to drive his opponent to the floor. His opponent has no option but to catch his weight with his hands, otherwise, he may by rolled over as he falls forward out of balance. This is all that the guerrilla needs to attack. As soon as the arm becomes available and is beyond the defensive perimeter of his opponent's body, it should be swiftly attacked. For SITREP 5.0, this results in a crafty rolling omoplata, though it could just as easily be a straight armlock or kimura.

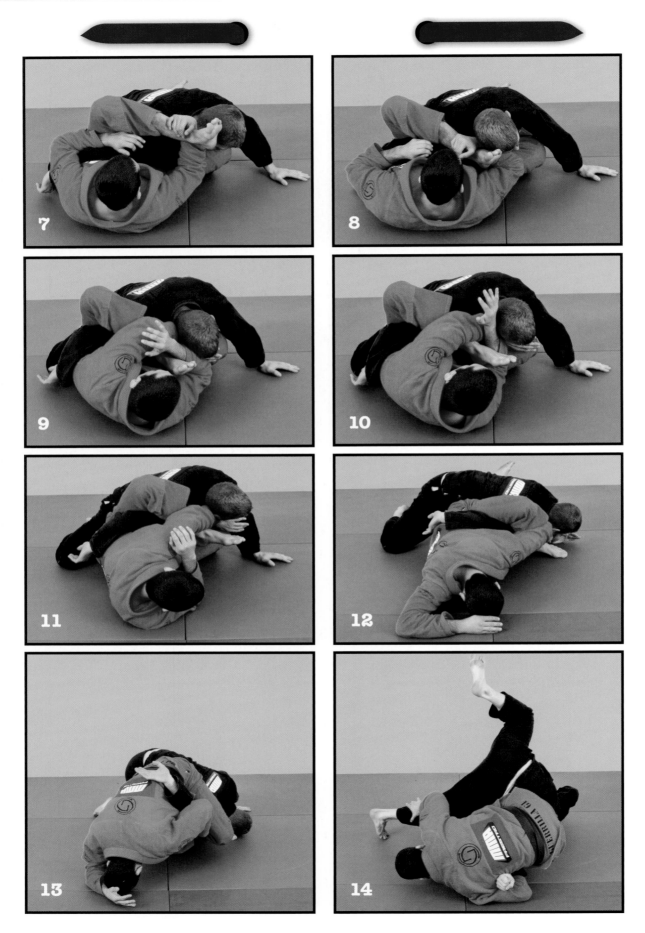

Plan of Attack:

a. SUBJECT CAMARILLO begins attacking CONTACT DARCY, MATTHEW within his closed guard. Already, Camarillo has swiped Darcy's arms to the outside and is bucking his hips forward to break Darcy's posture and to close the distance. The power of Camarillo's legs and hips is too much for Darcy to resist.

b. As a result of this action, Darcy must touch his hands to the mat for him to regain his posture and composure, and Camarillo realizes that. He immediately goes for the obvious attack—Darcy's right arm, which is nearest to Camarillo's head.

c. While maintaining control over Darcy's left wrist, Camarillo hip escapes to his left and circles his left arm counterclockwise over Darcy's right arm to trap it underneath his armpit. At this point, Darcy cannot easily regain his posture and he definitely feels an elevated threat level regarding his right arm.

d. Camarillo then circles his left leg clockwise over Darcy's right shoulder to enter an omoplata-style of control. To assist his left leg's flexibility, Camarillo hooks his right hand over his shin to help pull his leg in front of Darcy's face.

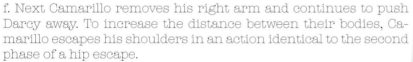

e. Before removing his arm, Camarillo expertly makes a ninety-degree frame with his right arm while his left hand reaches under his right to further push Darcy away. This prevents Darcy from closing the distance with Camarillo and keeps Darcy at an optimal angle of attack.

f. Next Camarillo removes his right arm and continues to push Darcy away. To increase the distance between their bodies, Camarillo escapes his shoulders in an action identical to the second phase of a hip escape.

g. Now, Camarillo can change course. He brings his right elbow underneath his body. This allows him to turn facedown toward the mat. His left pushing arm now clamps down on Darcy's elbow while still providing a block against any type of stacking or pressing movement.

h. Camarillo catches Darcy's right leg with his right hand and then tucks his left shouder into the mat. This disrupts Darcy's balance and forces him to forward roll. Camarillo guides Darcy's leg to the bottom SAP.

i. Before he lands, Darcy is already in a very tight modified juji gatame. Of special note is how this variation adds a level of twist to the submission to make it a hybrid shoulder-armlock. Darcy is forced to submit.

SNAFU MOMENT:

When pulling the leg over and attacking the obvious arm, the guerrilla must be prepared to deal with an opponent trying to step over his bottom leg. In this case, the framework provides an ideal block, as it disrupts the ability of the top fighter to close distance and step over the bottom leg. If the opponent does try to step over, the guerrilla should maintain a face-to-face angle and never return to his back, which would lead to a possible guard pass. Avoid the flat back at all costs!

AFTER-ACTION REPORT:

By deflecting the arms to the outside and using his hips to project the opponent forward the guerrilla leaves his opponent with no other option but to catch his collapse with his hands on the mat. Anytime the opponent's hands hit the mat, he is exposed for the attack. Whenever this occurs he must be attacked with a direct attack. This, of course, may lead to other counters and submissions, but at least it will make the guerrilla lead the fight instead of catch up to it.

SECTION TWO: Attacking the Periphery

Although indirect or peripheral attacks have been brought up throughout this study, it is important to give them their due attention. These attacks do more to confuse and disrupt the opponent than almost any other. All peripheral attacks focus on one element: attacking one side of the body to expose another. How this plays out can vary depending on the situation.

For instance, in order to expose an arm or neck in the guard, the opponent may wish to kick out the opponent's leg, wait for him to catch his balance, and then attack while he is in a state of confusion. While on top, this plays out much differently. Sometimes, the best way to get to a choke hold from the back is to focus on putting both hooks in to control the back. When the opponent invariably reaches down to deflect the hook, his neck is exposed for the attack. The same is true for the mounted and knee-on-belly positions. As the opponent seeks to push the knee or foot into the half guard, the guerrilla can again attack the neck or exposed arm.

In this regard, the guerrilla always looks at his opponent's body as having ample opportunities for attack. He can attack one arm with the goal of getting to the other. He may go after an upper-body attack to expose the lower body. Either way, by diverting the attention toward another area, the guerrilla is best able to expose his true target and finish it in the easiest and most direct attack.

SITREP 5.1 - ATTACKING THE BASE TO EXPOSE THE ARM

SITREP 5.0 used an indirect or peripheral action of unbalancing to expose the defender's arm for attack and SITREP 5.1 showcases how to attack the opponent's base with the aim of attacking the arm. In this situation, the combat base of the opponent prevents the guerrilla's hips and pelvis from reaching the armpit. By eliminating the knee that is in the way (through the shin-to-shin hook and extension), the guerrilla is able to freely attack the exposed arm.

Plan of Attack:

a. SUBJECT CAMARILLO is using the open guard against CONTACT DARCY, MATTHEW. Darcy has one knee up in a staggered combat base for balance. For control, Camarillo has a standard collar and sleeve grip and has just inserted his lower left shin in front of Darcy's basing right leg while his right foot rests on Darcy's left knee.

b. Instead of attacking the arm against Darcy's strong posture, Camarillo attacks the periphery by falling to his back and extending his left leg while he "gas pedals" Darcy's left knee. By straightening his left hooking leg, Camarillo is able to drop Darcy's base to the floor. As he does this, he pulls on his grips to further disrupt Darcy's equilibrium.

c. Now Darcy is focusing on regaining his posture and not on how exposed he is to attack. Camarillo releases his hook and turns his hips to face Darcy's now exposed right arm.

d. Camarillo slides his left shin over the right side of Darcy's neck, hooking his left foot behind the head. Then, Camarillo moves both of his arms to Darcy's limb in a standard armbar position.

e. It's too late for any defense. Camarillo rolls clockwise onto his left hip and finishes with a hips-facing armbar. Darcy is forced to tap from hyperextension as Camarillo drives his hips into Darcy's elbow and pulls at the wrist.

SNAFU MOMENT—FORGETTING THE GAS PEDAL:

The guerrilla must be sure to use the gas pedal on the knee along with the hook. Without this, some opponents will be able to pop their knees back into the original position. Instead, use the gas pedal along with a pulling motion as a roadblock to trip the opponent forward as his basing leg is extended forward.

AFTER-ACTION REPORT:

Grappling can be seen as the removal of obstacles on the way to securing one's personal objective. In SITREP 5.1, the obstacle is the opponent's knee that blocks the attack on the exposed arm. By getting rid of this nuisance, the guerrilla is able to instantly attack the arm and finish the fight. If he had attacked without removing the lower-body obstacle, he would likely have been countered and may have had his guard passed as a result.

Regarding the finishing phase, it is important that the guerrilla hooks the opponent's head as he rolls into the hips-facing armbar. If he clears his opponent's face with his leg while moving into the position, he will lose the opportunity to control the head. This control is very helpful in situations where the opponent tries to jump over the body to defend the submission.

SECTION THREE: Skill Development

It can be said that all indirect or peripheral attacks lead to obvious submissions and that many obvious submissions rely on an indirect attack for exposure. However, both indirect and direct attacks are worthless without proper skill and timing in getting to the position, feint, or finish. This is where skill development becomes necessary for the guerrilla.

When it comes to skill development there are three areas that are king: static uchikomis (or nonresistant drills for repetition), progressive resistance uchikomis, and situational sparring.

During static uchikomis, the attacker is able to develop the speed, timing, and body mechanics that are necessary for successful implementation.

Progressive resistance uchikomis teach the attacker to be heavier and tighter in the follow-through so he can learn what it feels like to be successful in the submission. These can range from small to medium amounts of resistance with the goal of developing positional control.

Situational sparring is where the newly developed skill best gets put to work. Through situational sparring, the attacker gets many looks at the target and has multiple chances to apply the skill in a sparring context.

By combining all three elements, the guerrilla ensures that he will be ready to spring when the direct or obvious attack presents itself. If failure occurs, he also knows what he must drill to ensure that the mistake is not repeated.

SITREP 5.2 - CLOSED GUARD ARMBAR UCHIKOMI

The closed guard armbar uchikomi is the starting and returning place for most skill development and troubleshooting. This drill teaches all of the proper mechanics to control the arm, bring the hips to the armpit, get to a proper attack angle, off-balance the opponent, and finish. This should be the first drill to return to for those guerrillas who are struggling with their entries, control, and finish. This movement also adapts well to single-leg defense, jumping attacks, and the open guard, all of which rely on a stronger pull and hip-to-armpit action.

Plan of Attack:

a. SUBJECT CAMARILLO begins the armbar uchikomi drill with CONTACT DARCY, MATTHEW within his closed guard. Camarillo is controlling the same side sleeve with his left hand while his right arm cross-grips to trap Darcy's right triceps. This triceps grip acts as a "backstop" to prevent Darcy from pulling his arm backward.

b. Camarillo places his left foot on Darcy's hip, pinches his left knee tight to Darcy to prevent any gaps, and pushes off to move his head toward Darcy's left knee. At the same time, he lifts his right foot high into Darcy's left armpit for control and to drive Darcy off balance.

c. From this perpendicular angle, it is easy to continue this motion and snap his left foot over Darcy's head for the armbar. Camarillo does not overly extend the elbow because his goal is to drill crisp repetitions and not to exhaust his partner's elbows.

d. To continue the drill, Camarillo swings his left foot in a counterclockwise arc. The weight of his left foot pulls his body back into a square guard position. Already, Camarillo is switching his grips to prepare for the other side.

e. Continuing the momentum from his arcing foot, Camarillo now throws his right leg in a similar arc to bring his hips beneath Darcy's left elbow. With the grips already in place, Camarillo is in great position to finish another armbar for the drill.

f. Camarillo snaps his right leg over Darcy's head and will continue the drill by now arcing his foot clockwise, alternating his grips, and attacking the right arm.

SNAFU MOMENT:

The real SNAFU while drilling armbars is laziness, apathy, and a lack of snap. The guerrilla drills every move perfectly and is careful to drill proper form and high hips to ensure that the arm is completely under control. Having low hips leads to armbar escapes and drilling bad form leads to multiple SNAFUs in sparring and competition.

AFTER-ACTION REPORT:

Once confidence is built in the movement phase of static uchikomi, the attacker should move to progressive resistance to make sure his legs are securing every single step of the movement. Great movement is always the ideal, but great movement and a lack of control or tightness in the armbar can be a fatal flaw, especially in bottom armbars where weight, pressure, and passing defense can wear down even the greatest grapplers.

SITREP 5.3 - KNEE-ON-BELLY ARMBAR UCHIKOMI

The knee-on-belly armbar uchikomi is an excellent drill not only for its finishing aspect, but also because it includes a transition into both the side control and knee-on-belly and finishes with the submission. This makes this movement a must-drill for everyone. Regarding the finish, the guerrilla must master the slide from the knee-on-belly to the shin in the armpit. This critical point will determine overall success or failure when applied against a fully resisting opponent.

Plan of Attack:

a. SUBJECT CAMARILLO begins the knee-on-belly armbar drill from the top of CONTACT DARCY, MATTHEW. Camarillo is in the side control with his left hand gripping Darcy's left shoulder and his right hand gripping Darcy's left hip.

b. Camarillo springs off the floor and slides his right knee across Darcy's abdomen, filling the void between Darcy and himself.

c. Next, Camarillo grips Darcy's near-side arm with his left hand and his right hand posts his weight on Darcy's left shoulder. This prevents Darcy's escape, stifles his hip movement, and exposes the arm for attack. To get to the finishing position, Camarillo slides his right shin into Darcy's armpit.

d. With his right shin tight to the armpit, Camarillo only needs to step his left foot over Darcy's face and fall back to get to the armbar finish. As with the previous drill, Camarillo goes easy on his partner's elbow to ensure many more repetitions.

e. Maintaining his grips, Camarillo steps his left leg back and leans forward to Darcy's body. Camarillo continuously pulls the arm throughout the movement to ensure control.

f. Camarillo returns to the side control and is ready to renew the drill with his next repetition.

g. Camarillo pops his hips upward in a similar fashion as a surfer standing up on a wave and is ready to move to his next near-side armbar.

Just as the closed guard armbar uchikomi relies on high hips, the knee-on-belly armbar uchikomi should be drilled with the goal of getting the shin tight to the armpit along with a strong pull for exposure. To attempt to just fall back into the armbar from a standard knee-on-belly without moving the shin high is more than a SNAFU, it is PP (poor preparation) and not an attribute of guerrilla training.

AFTER-ACTION REPORT:

The knee-on-belly uchikomi is a great movement to practice along with a favorite guard pass or from a side control starting point because it links more than one position and it ends in a high-percentage submission from the knee-on-belly.

As stated earlier, the shin in the armpit is everything for the success of this attack, but to get to the armpit, the guerrilla should have a strong pull on the near-side arm and adequate pressure to make the opponent give up the limb.

SITREP 5.4 - ARMBAR FROM BACK UCHIKOMI

The armbar from the back uchikomi is often a difficult transition for new grapplers, but it includes a movement phase that makes it more practical for static uchikomis than drilling rear-naked chokes with the back hooks. To be successful, the guerrilla should belt-line hook, kimura lock, and then use both the foot and the kimura lock to push the opponent to his back. This will ensure that the guerrilla will fall back into an armlock from the SAP instead of pulling the defender to the top position.

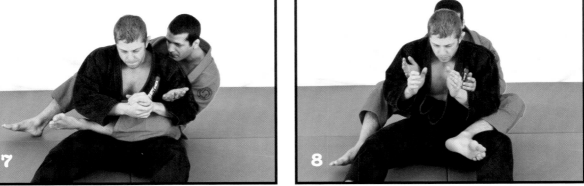

Plan of Attack:

a. SUBJECT CAMARILLO begins the armbar from the back uchikomi in the back position with CONTACT DARCY, MATTHEW. Camarillo has angled his lower left leg into a belt-line hook and has underhooked Darcy's left arm.

b. Next Camarillo reaches over Darcy's left shoulder with his right hand and secures a figure-four lock by grabbing Darcy's left wrist with his right hand while his left hand grabs his own right wrist.

c. In a two-part motion, Camarillo swings his right leg over Darcy's face and then drives the figure-four lock into Darcy's chest while his right leg pushes into Darcy's face. This drastically inhibits Darcy's ability to pressure into Camarillo.

d. The push of Camarillo's leg and arm entanglement drive Darcy to his back and into a finishing SAP. At this point, Camarillo can now fall back into the armbar.

e. Instead of falling into the armlock, Camarillo rocks back and swings his right leg clockwise off Darcy's head. He follows the momentum of the leg as Darcy sits up.

f. This momentum carries Camarillo back to the move's origin with Camarillo on the back with a strong belt-line hook for control. Immediately, Camarillo will execute a second repetition.

SNAFU MOMENT—PULLING THE ARM:

When the guerrilla drills getting to the kimura and then armbar, he should never pull the arm until his opponent is on his back. Instead, drill to use the kimura and leg to push the opponent to his back and then pull for the armbar once on the back. If the guerrilla drills to pull immediately on the arm, he will find many opponents pushing him either into the guard or to a back-on-the-floor armbar.

AFTER-ACTION REPORT:

As with any static uchikomi, the movement phase is most important. For the armbar from the back, the kimura takes the brunt of the work as it both isolates the arm and controls the opponent's posture.

During progressive resistance uchikomis, the guerrilla should test his ability to push both the kimura lock and his leg over the face into the opponent. The goal is to push him to his back while the defender fights vigorously to get to his knees. This is the fight as it will happen and it is an important feeling and skill for the guerrilla to develop before he ever gets to the real fight.

CONFIDENTIAL INFORMATION

Attack, Withdrawal, Ambush & Retreat

FILE 006: ATTACK, WITHDRAWAL, AMBUSH, & RETREAT

The guerrilla grappler must remember that he is always a guerrilla at heart. He should use the elements of attack and withdrawal, ambush, and retreat to effectively frustrate and eventually finish any opponent. He must remember that most guerrillas fight against greater forces and must use their tactics wisely to be successful on the battlefield. The guerrilla grappler should seek the same tactics when overwhelmed, outmatched, and underpowered.

Through attack and withdrawal, the guerrilla uses speed to get in and out of attack range to test and batter the opponent's defense. As soon as a weakness is felt, it is time to attack relentlessly.

For the ambush, it is critical that the guerrilla does not chase an advantaged opponent. Instead, he familiarizes himself with leading the opponent toward his greatest weapon. This maximizes the guerrilla's ability to fight off even the best adversary.

Guerrillas are not invulnerable and if their ambushes fail, they should move to a defendable position. This is where retreat comes into play. Running from a fight in war leads to bullets in the back and the same can be said for running from a dangerous grappler. Instead, the guerrilla learns to retreat actively by fighting to get to his preferred position to launch a counterstrike.

Every guerrilla grappler should hold these ideals true and learn to fight in both the best and worst situations to overcome even the most awe-inspiring opponents.

SECTION ONE: Biting Like Fleas...

The tactic of constantly attacking and withdrawing or nipping away at the opponent can never be overlooked or understated. This nuisance phase of grappling has great psychological effect on the opponent as the guerrilla bites like fleas at his defenses.

Although this constant attack and withdrawal type of guerrilla warfare is not meant to directly cause a submission per se, it often leads to ambush and other opportunities for attack as the opponent grows frustrated and loses his cool. In addition, these small, fast, and plentiful actions are a great way to test the opponent's defense and feel him out for weaknesses in strength or positioning.

SECTION TWO: Ambush

The ambush is the fruit of proper preparation and it is the easiest submission to execute. Again, the guerrilla grappler should focus on the five Ps: Planning and Preparation Prevent Poor Performance. Though it may seem difficult to plan for an ambush in the heat of an intense grappling exchange, it is possible with proper baiting and technical foresight.

For the budding ambusher, it is important to think of the funnel web spider and the patience and time it takes to create a complex web and hide it from its prey. Only when the web is ready does the spider begin its waiting game for its next meal. When the unsuspecting victim comes along and falls into the deadly trap it is immediately consumed. What is true for the arachnid is true for the grappler.

Focusing on human adversaries, the idea remains the same. It is only the context of the bait or trap that changes. With an ambushing mindset, a guerrilla may present an arm to be grabbed easily. When the opponent blunders forward to grip the arm, he springs the trap and is immediately sucked into a triangle lock or reversed. The guerrilla may present his knee to the stand-up fighter or wrestler and when the opponent jumps for the single-leg, he answers with a reversal or submission.

Regardless of the bait or booby trap, the guerrilla must hide his intention and be prepared to launch the ambush at a moment's notice! This is key to developing one of the easiest submissions in the world—the submission that the opponent willingly walks into.

SECTION THREE: Retreat

Though attack and withdrawal may lead an opponent into a devastating ambush, there is always the chance that the opponent will never take the bait and press forward with his own attacking game plan or possibly overwhelm the ambush with greater physical force. In these circumstances, retreat becomes the best option.

By retreating, the guerrilla does not lose but instead leaves a situation that is untenable in order to establish a situation where he can counterattack and renew his offense. If the guerrilla has nearly been bucked off the mount and is in danger of being put in an opponent's dangerous guard, perhaps it is better to retreat back to the closed guard, where he may have a greater opportunity to finish the fight.

This takes familiarity with grappling, experience dealing with the many different types of grapplers and their strong suits, and an honesty regarding personal strengths and weaknesses. If a guerrilla knows his best position is the side control, he should retreat from the knee-on-belly to the side control where he can best dominate and secure the submission.

The guerrilla must consider retreat as a parachute, and must prepare his parachute to deploy every time it is needed so that he will arrive in his fallback position with the best possible control. To do this, he must fight to break grips as he retreats in order to land in position ready to counterattack for the victory. Passive retreating will often lead to a change in momentum as the opponent presses forward with his own attacks or escape game plan, therefore it is vital to retreat with consistent aggression and purpose.

SITREP 6.0 - RETREAT TO CLOSED GUARD

Though there are many ways to finish from the SAP, there is always the chance that a strong or more experienced grappler will manage to escape explosively. In this situation, the guerrilla must recognize whether he should stay with the submission, stay on top, or retreat into the guard position. In SITREP 6.0, the opponent has overwhelmed the SAP, but instead of falling to guard, the guerrilla actively fights to pull the opponent's arms into the closed guard position so he will then be in position to counter and go back on the offensive.

SUBMIT EVERYONE

Plan of Attack:

a. SUBJECT CAMARILLO has reached the head-side SAP against CONTACT DARCY, MATTHEW. Darcy is incredibly wary of Camarillo's arm attacks and has already pushed Camarillo's leg off his face. Darcy's goal is to drive his weight over the leg to inhibit the finish and set up an escape path.

b. Darcy successfully drives his weight over Camarillo's leg and is correctly bridging his weight onto the leg to pin it, restricting Camarillo's ability to move efficiently and counter the escape.

c. To take advantage of the escape, Darcy immediately turns into Camarillo and starts rushing into his guard. As he does so, Camarillo abandons any notion of the armlock and instead insists on pulling Darcy's right elbow toward him.

d. The pulling action brings Darcy's arms inside of Camarillo's guard. Although he lost the top position, he was able to retreat on his terms and get to a more positive platform to renew his attacks.

SNAFU MOMENT:

Any escape for the opponent is a SNAFU for the guerrilla attacker. Every single one. However, the guerrilla must be prepared for this eventuality and must actively retreat to ensure that he arrives at either a neutral or in the best case scenario, favorable position to attack. The guerrilla can never lazily accept the escape or else he may face the changing tides of battle.

AFTER-ACTION REPORT:

Reading the opponent and making that instant judgment is key for the experienced guerrilla grappler. In SITREP 6.0, SUBJECT CAMARILLO had to decide in an instant if he could continue the arm attack, try to fight for the mount or side control, or actively retreat to a position where he still felt strong. In the end, he chose to move into one of his most dangerous positions, the closed guard. This ability to decide on the fly is of the utmost importance and is a hallmark of good battlefield decision making, preservation, and future success.

DO NOT ATTEMPT

If the guerrilla fails to pull on the arms and just falls into the guard, he may fall into a favorable passing position for his opponent. Always retreat aggressively!

CONFIDENTIAL INFORMATION

1209-83-68-888

Creating Chaos & Psychological Operations

FILE 007: PSYCHOLOGICAL OPERATIONS

It often has been said that all fighting is 90% mental and 10% physical, though it is likely that it is far more mental than even this. Whether it is in warfare, guerrilla tactics, the local grappling tournament, or the cage, every fighter can benefit from focusing on the mental aspects of the game, including how to control and effect the opponent's attitude and overall state of being. If the guerrilla can lead an opponent into emotions that are outside of his comfort zone, he is more likely to make mistakes, and these are the mistakes that a guerrilla loves to capitalize on with a well-executed submission.

To this end, the guerrilla grappler's psychological operations include creating chaos—the overall systematic shutdown of an opponent due to constant movement and stimulus, and the more broadly defined Psy Ops, which focus on lie detection, prediction, and tempo control to beat an opponent down mentally through grappling technique.

Unmentioned is the creation of the self, the identity of the guerrilla grappler as one who is able to overcome great pain, hardship, and mental and physical discomfort to achieve his prescribed task. This comes through training, persistence, and an almost fanatical insistence on succeeding where others fail.

For the guerrilla, the culmination of a strong "self" through experience and perseverance is a nearly unstoppable weapon when combined with the psychological operations herein. Woe to the unsuspecting grappler that believes technique or strength will ever be more powerful than a driven and dedicated mind.

SECTION ONE: Creating Chaos

Chaos should be seen as grappling's poststructuralism. It is a revolution against grappling norms and it often flies in the face of well-established pedagogy. Creating chaos happens whenever a grappler willingly leaves the orthodoxy of a certain grappling curriculum to confuse and frustrate his opponent. Like it or not, most grapplers fall in line regarding what is "normal" grappling behavior, and this norm can be used to hinder a grappler's senses.

For the guerrilla grappler, creating chaos works to confuse the opponent's defenses, making it easier to sneak an attack through. This chaos can be categorized by several different approaches, but the most obvious are overstimulus and random change.

Through overstimulus, the guerrilla attempts to bombard his opponent with not one or two actions but three, four, five, and more actions that come from many different angles. In doing so, the guerrilla overwhelms his opponent's nervous system, as he is unable to react to all the different stimuli. The intensity of this bombardment is compounded by the use of unorthodox movements that leave the opponent even more frustrated and unclear as to how to approach or defend the attack.

Random change also relies on unorthodox movements, but it is particular to situations where the opponent feels certain that the guerrilla will react with a certain programmed response. It is then that the opponent loses everything as the guerrilla changes paths. To the opponent, this feels like random change and this is where the name originates, though for the guerrilla it is anything but random. It is methodical and it is for the benefit of mental domination.

When combined, overstimulation and random change work great to overwhelm the senses and leave the opponent exhausted, frustrated, and ready to be finished.

SITREP 7.0 - GUERRILLA TORNADO TO ARMBAR

SITREP 7.0 is an excellent example of using overstimulus to create chaos during the guard pass and subsequent armbar finish. Through the use of an unorthodox spin pass, the guerrilla leaves the opponent unclear as to how to defend. By the time the opponent tries to turn to face his back, the guerrilla is already on his side. When the opponent realizes he should turn toward the knee-on-belly, it is also too late, for the guerrilla has already crossed over the body and is attacking the arm. The opponent is left frazzled and in total shutdown.

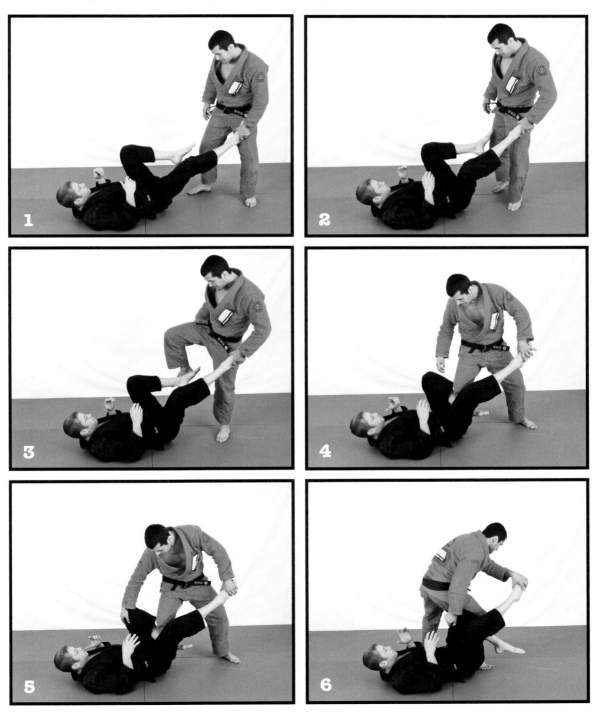

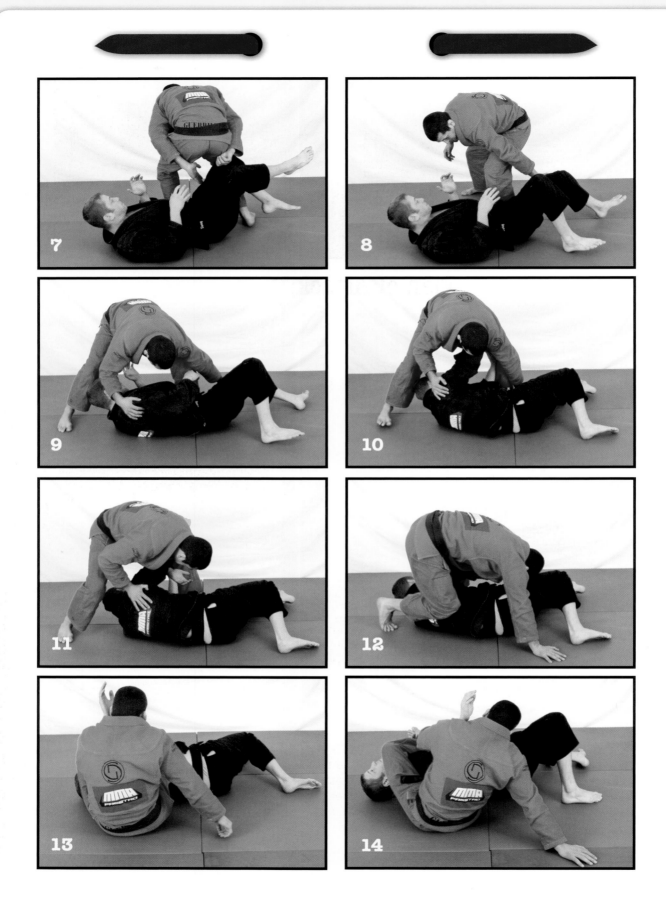

SUBMIT EVERYONE

Plan of Attack:

a. SUBJECT CAMARILLO approaches the open guard of CONTACT DARCY, MATTHEW. As he nears Darcy's legs, he controls the right foot with his left hand.

b. Instead of stepping one leg inside of his guard as is typical of many jiu-jitsu practitioners, Camarillo steps his right shin in front of and into Darcy's left shin. Camarillo then presses his shin forward to pin Darcy's left heel to his rear. This immobilizes Darcy's entire left leg. As this occurs, Camarillo guides Darcy's left leg to the outside.

c. Then, Camarillo grips Darcy's left knee with his right hand and takes a backward counterclockwise step with his left foot. Though Darcy would love to attack the back, the motion is incredibly rapid and Camarillo's control over his legs eliminates that threat.

d. Camarillo does not stop his spin as he continues his counterclockwise turn, stepping his right foot to the outside and arriving in a near knee-on-belly position. At this point, Camarillo only controls Darcy's left knee to prevent his hip movement or leg entanglement.

e. Even then, Camarillo does not quit with his confusing spin. He steps his right leg over Darcy's head and releases his grips for balance. With his grips out of the picture, Darcy instinctively turns toward him to escape.

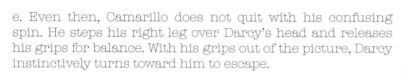

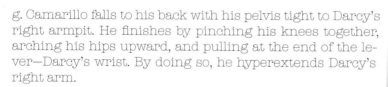

f. By continuing his original counterclockwise turn, Camarillo has deftly shifted his body into position for the juji gatame. Camarillo catches Darcy's right elbow in the snare.

g. Camarillo falls to his back with his pelvis tight to Darcy's right armpit. He finishes by pinching his knees together, arching his hips upward, and pulling at the end of the lever—Darcy's wrist. By doing so, he hyperextends Darcy's right arm.

AFTER-ACTION REPORT:

In this case the spinning action works to confuse the opponent and this confusion plays to the guerrilla's advantage. Although the opponent feels like there is nothing but chaos surrounding him, the guerrilla is in complete control because this was a part of his plan of action from the outset. The plan? Use chaos to create an opening for the submission.

SITREP 7.1 - SAME-SIDE ARMDRAG TO JUJI ROLL

SITREP 7.1 is an excellent showcase of random change and how this creates chaos for the opponent. When armdragged, most opponents focus on defending their backs, protecting against a rear lapel choke, or a fall to the guard armbar. This reaction is drilled into most submission wrestlers and jiu-jitsu practitioners. So instead of following this norm, the guerrilla thinks outside the box and attacks a rolling juji-gatame to catch the opponent completely off guard. Random change creates chaos and ends in the submission.

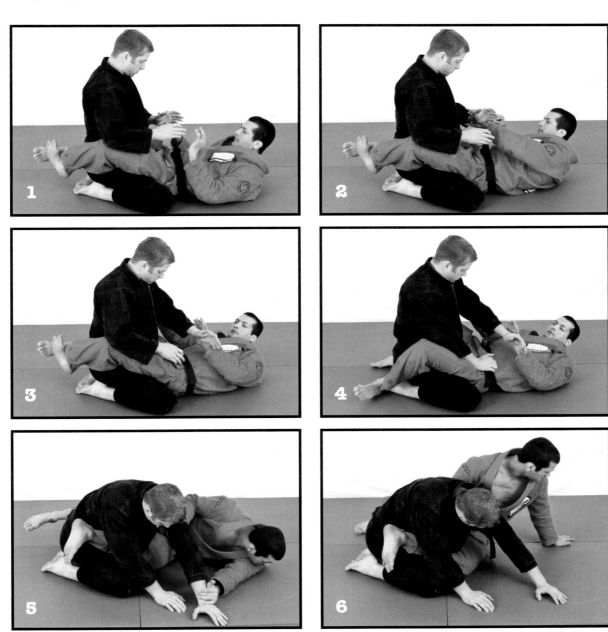

Plan of Attack:

a. SUBJECT CAMARILLO begins with CONTACT DARCY, MATTHEW inside of his closed guard. Already Camarillo has circled his right hand to Darcy's left elbow and his left hand is on the outside of Darcy's left wrist.

b. In one explosive movement Camarillo hip escapes away from Darcy and pushes Darcy's elbow and wrist away. This puts Camarillo on the outside and exposes Darcy's back.

c. Camarillo bases out with his left hand. This provides a good defense against Darcy trying to push his way toward Camarillo to prevent his back from being taken. Camarillo continues to push against Darcy's left elbow and triceps.

d. Camarillo confuses Darcy, who is only expecting the traditional back attack. He points his knee downward and projects his hips over Darcy's armpit, not his back. Camarillo is completely facing the arm!

e. Then, Camarillo slides his right shin over the back of Darcy's neck and hugs the exposed left arm with his own right arm. Camarillo makes a strong hook against Darcy's neck that helps him to push Darcy's neck forward.

f. To finish, Camarillo shoots his right knee under his body so that he lands on his hip. Now, Camarillo pulls at the wrist and thrusts his hips toward Darcy's hips while arching his back to hyperextend Darcy's elbow.

SNAFU MOMENT—JUMPING FOR THE ARM WITHOUT BASE:

The guerrilla must base out with one arm before going for his opponent's arm. Otherwise, he will be too close to the mat and unable to deal with his partner pressing forward. This posting arm also helps the guerrilla gain altitude to push his hips higher so that he is careful to clear his opponent's shoulders as he moves from a possible back attack to an armbar submission.

AFTER-ACTION REPORT:

Random change is a fascinating facet of chaos creation and should be used at any point the guerrilla thinks it will create an obvious advantage over "norm" techniques. This is not to say that fundamentals should be ignored. Instead, the intentions and experiences of the opponent have to be taken into consideration and each grappling match should be treated as the dynamic stream of consciousness that it is.

SECTION TWO: Psy Ops

Psy Ops are the second level of operations that must be used for all successful attackers and guerrilla grapplers. These psychological operations work almost like mind control in that they are so strong that the guerrilla may actually feel like he is reading his opponent's mind. The elements of Psy-Ops are prediction, tempo control, and lie detection.

The first element is prediction, and it is based on the ability of the guerrilla to make high-percentage guesses as to his opponent's next set of movements. These are usually based on of anatomical possibilities (e.g., an opponent on the bottom of side control can only escape to the left and right) and scouting/past records. For example, if an opponent has a history of pulling the half guard, the guerrilla may wish to either hide his leg from the guard and pass or pull guard himself, thereby taking the opponent out of his game plan.

Tempo control is the second element of Psy-Ops and it focuses on reading the opponent's mood and changing the tempo or adjusting the speed or pressure of the match to counteract the pace at which the opponent would like to operate. Again, this keeps the opponent off guard and out of his comfort area.

Finally there is lie detection or the understanding of an opponent's real intentions. This helps a guerrilla to understand when an attack is real and when it is a feint. It is the accumulation of scouting, experience, and mat time, and it is something that can be felt as well as seen. Regarding lie detection, if a guerrilla correctly deduces that the opponent's attack is halfhearted, it is over, and this is one of the most obvious mental differences between high- and low-level grapplers.

For the novice and professional, these tools must be honed along with the basics, fire bases, and fire teams to ensure total mental, technical, and physical domination.

SITREP 7.2 - PREDICTION OF GAME TYPE

An essential part of prediction that comes with grappling experience is prediction based on game type. In SITREP 7.2, the guerrilla is clearly in an advantageous position and he is facing a flexible opponent with great hip mobility and a good guard. Therefore, the guerrilla is prepared for the opponent to use his hip flexibility and guard retention skills to recover the guard. Since the guerrilla has seen and felt this type of recovery, he hides his hands so that the opponent recovers into a passable guard instead of an active one.

Plan of Attack:

a. SUBJECT CAMARILLO is attempting to take the back against CONTACT DARCY, MATTHEW, but Darcy has a very persistent hip escaping movement. To combat this, Camarillo hooks his left foot behind Darcy's left knee and projects his legs forward, away from his escaping movement.

b. This puts Darcy in a position where he is more exposed to have his back taken and allows Camarillo to add some top pressure with his chest against Darcy's shoulder.

c. Darcy does not like where this is headed and explosively pushes off the mat with his right foot in an inverting movement not unlike the wrestler's Granby roll. Camarillo has been here before and removes his left arm by circling it underneath Darcy's hips. With this one small movement, Camarillo changes everything for Darcy.

d. Instead of escaping to a guard position, Darcy is now in a stacked position with Camarillo already pressing Darcy's left knee toward his face.

e. Camarillo drives further forward and shows patience, allowing his body weight to create great discomfort for Darcy as his diaphragm is compressed, restricting his breathing. Camarillo uses his left arm as a guide for the other hip, always guiding Darcy into greater pain while his right forearm starts to choke Darcy with his hand in Darcy's right collar.

f. The pressure is too much, and Darcy kicks his left leg to the right to allow Camarillo to pass his guard. Even from here, the choke is still creating problems for Darcy.

g. Camarillo arrives in the side control and maintains control over the hips and choke in case Darcy attempts the same inverted roll escape.

SNAFU MOMENT—NOT HIDING THE ARM AGAINST GRANBY ROLLS:

Wrestlers have been hitting the Granby roll defense for years and years, and it always works effectively by slamming the hips and body into the attacker's arm to throw the weight of the attacker forward to the mat. A guerrilla must predict when his opponent will try to execute this type of inverted movement; usually it is flexible opponents. By hiding his arm, the guerrilla forces the escapee to only land in more trouble and an easy guard pass.

AFTER-ACTION REPORT:

Prediction takes on many different aspects, and one that comes with scouting is game-type awareness. Even without this, the guerrilla may still be savvy enough to hide his arms as the guard is recovered and may yet pass, but the earlier this is recognized, the more likely it is that the guerrilla will stay in dominant control and remain more than a few steps ahead of his desperate opponent.

Psychologically, this creates frustration and later resignation in the opponent as his go-to maneuvers are continually blocked. As in SITREP 7.2, there is a feeling of helplessness as the guard is easily passed.

SITREP 7.3 - PREDICTION FROM COMMONALITIES

SITREP 7.3 is different from SITREP 7.2 in that it is not based solely on a particular individual's style of escaping, but a more common escape that most grapplers are aware of. For this example, the guard recovery from the north-south is analyzed. What the guerrilla must recognize is the needs of the escapee. By straightening his arms, the opponent is hoping to make enough space to fill with his bent legs for the escape. With this in mind, the guerrilla can create a game plan to stop the knees from entering and then simply knee-slice pass to the side control.

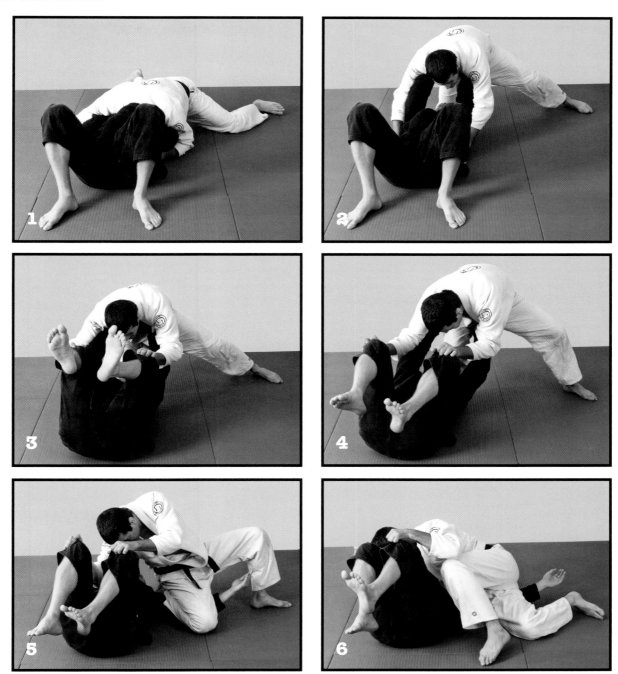

Plan of Attack:

a. SUBJECT CAMARILLO begins having already reached the north-south pin against CONTACT DARCY, MATTHEW. Camarillo is pinning his weight forward while grasping Darcy's belt at the hip level. Darcy has his hands tucked inside of Camarillo's and will use this to escape.

b. Explosively, Darcy pushes Camarillo away with both hands as he tries to tuck his knees inside of his elbows to escape. Camarillo predicts that this is Darcy's POE and defends first by pushing against Darcy's knees and secondly by slicing his right knee over Darcy's left arm, essentially eliminating both Darcy's pushing hands and penetrating knees.

c. Camarillo continues the knee-slice, driving his body to the left side control position of Darcy. Again, Camarillo maintains control of the near-side leg to ensure that Darcy will not be attempting another escape.

SNAFU MOMENT—MOVEMENT:

The guerrilla on top must keep the bottom player in the same position. It is essential that he limits the amount of backward roll that the opponent can commit to—if his lower back is stuck on the mat, he will be less mobile. Also, the guerrilla should track the opponent by pushing into his knees and circling him to stay in the same position until he is ready to knee-slice to side control. This keeps the opponent stuck and frustrated.

AFTER-ACTION REPORT:

By understanding the limited possibilities of the escapee as well as his personal needs, the guerrilla can predict his behavior and set up an easy counter. In this situation, the guerrilla only has to block his opponent's legs from entering between his opponent's torso and his own to prevent him from inverting into the guard recovery.

Though this appears and actually is quite simple, this rudimentary block should be very irritating for the bottom opponent, as he is stuck in limbo while watching his guard get passed yet again.

SITREP 7.4 - PREDICTION DUE TO LIMITING OPTIONS

For SITREP 7.4, the guerrilla successfully predicts the roll away from side control because he has set that up as the opponent's best option. In this case, the cross-face and hip block prevent the opponent from escaping toward the guerrilla, while the opponent's previous misadventure with inversion in SITREP 7.2 has him wary of that type of recovery. This leads the opponent to try to roll away in order to "run" from the side control. But it only provides the guerrilla with an opportunity to easily take his opponent's back, as he has channeled him toward this escape.

Plan of Attack:

a. SUBJECT CAMARILLO is on the top side control position against CONTACT DARCY, MATTHEW. Darcy is in a good defensive posture with his elbows inside of Camarillo's and locked firmly to his own torso. This will help dissuade Camarillo from attacking his arms. Camarillo faces Darcy's legs to set up a possible mount.

b. Darcy senses he may be mounted and explosively turns away from Camarillo. To slow Darcy, Camarillo controls his right arm while driving his elbow into Darcy's hip to better command the situation.

c. As Darcy fights to get to his knees, a gap opens between Darcy's right hip and the mat. Camarillo takes advantage of this by sliding his right leg inside the hole to get a bottom hook control.

d. Camarillo then hip escapes while pulling with his left arm to force Darcy to fall into his lap. Now, Camarillo slides his right arm over the shoulder to start attacking Darcy's neck with a choke. Camarillo makes sure to keep his head close to Darcy's ear to keep everything tight and secure.

e. With Darcy concerned about his neck and his defenses migrating toward his head, Camarillo has a clear shot to put his left leg in front of Darcy's left thigh to make a secondary hook to secure the back. Now, Camarillo can attack the choke with impunity.

SNAFU MOMENT:

If unable to secure the bottom arm to block the POE, secure *any* far-side control, whether it is the opposite side lapel or a far hip block. While neither may have the same submission implications, both will provide a transitional block inhibiting the opponent from reaching his knees. Regardless of the situation, the task is the same—do not allow the opponent to escape the attack zone.

AFTER-ACTION REPORT:

This area of prediction is based on limiting the opponent's options. With the cross-face and hip block in place, the opponent can only turn away, but the guerrilla is ready to slow him down with his grip control, and he has the grappling experience to understand that the bottom hook will come easily as the opponent tries to move to his knees to escape. In the end, the opponent feels like part of a herd of cattle, as he was helplessly corralled from one control to an even worse position and later submission.

SITREP 7.5 - COMBINING TEMPO CONTROL AND PREDICTION

In SITREP 7.5, the guerrilla has two aces up his sleeve. On the one hand, he uses prediction and grappling experience to understand that his opponent is trying to recover the guard from the turtle position. However, he also is controlling the tempo. Instead of waiting or slowing down for the recovery or to stall out the escape attempt, the guerrilla puts his engine into overdrive and passes the guard more aggressively than his opponent's guard recovery. The result is the guerrilla moving from a good position to a better top domination.

Plan of Attack:

a. SUBJECT CAMARILLO is in a situation to control the tempo against CONTACT DARCY, MATTHEW. While attacking from the top of the turtle, Darcy initiated an escape by hooking his left foot and shin on Camarillo's right hip and turning to pull Camarillo into the guard. Camarillo has transitioned his left hand from the waist to the knee to set up his counter-transition.

b. As Darcy sits through to the guard, Camarillo is already on his feet and moving toward Darcy's right side. Though Darcy has executed a great escape, he was not prepared for Camarillo to keep passing.

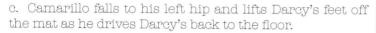

c. Camarillo falls to his left hip and lifts Darcy's feet off the mat as he drives Darcy's back to the floor.

d. To finish the counter, Camarillo steps his right leg deep underneath Darcy's right leg to immobilize Darcy's hip movement away from Camarillo. By controlling the tempo and using an attacking mindset, Camarillo is able to stay ahead of Darcy and get to an even better position.

SNAFU MOMENT—NEVER ALLOWING OPEN ELBOWS:

The guerrilla must never allow his elbows to be opened up. In this case, many opponents will try to pull on the elbow as they sit through to the guard, often leading to an omoplata or kimura and not just a successful guard pull. Therefore, the guerrilla always fights to keep his elbows to himself, make his own grips, and pass through any defensive counter.

AFTER-ACTION REPORT:

Prediction meets tempo control in this situation, but it cannot be overstated that prediction is not enough in such a situation. To be successful in this scenario, the guerrilla had to change his focus and adapt from a slow controlling tempo while on the back of the turtle to a rapid action. This idea of changing gears is important to all guerrillas, who should stifle their opponent's speed, win in a flat-out race, and stay in command of the pacing of the fight.

SITREP 7.6 - LIE DETECTION FLOW TRAINING

Defensive flow training is one of the best ways to recognize one of the most difficult aspects of Psy-Ops: lie detection. SITREP 7.6 is a great example of how flowing defensively out of repeated attacks can train the guerrilla's body to recognize when an action is a threat or simply a feint. By changing the intensity and pace, the guerrilla can focus on the sensation of threat training while a lighter flowing pace mimics the sensation of feints and fake attacks. Once armed with this body recognition, the guerrilla is far more likely to act decisively against varied threats.

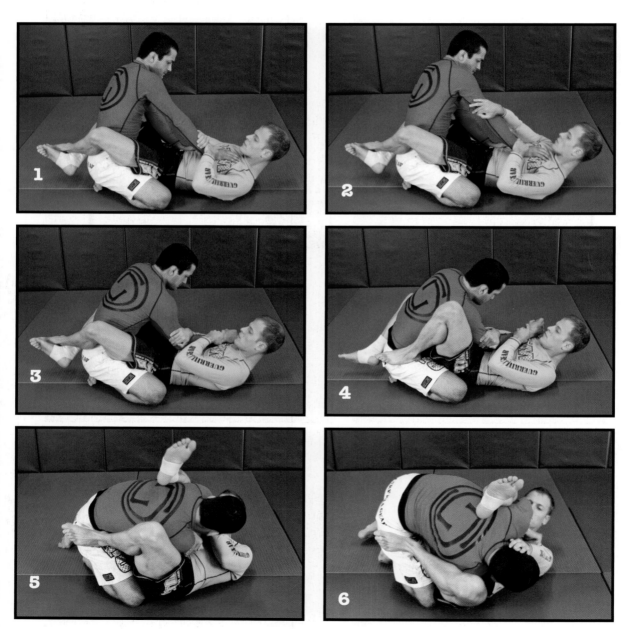

SUBMIT EVERYONE

Plan of Attack:

a. SUBJECT CAMARILLO begins the defensive drill within the closed guard of CONTACT FERRISS, TIMOTHY. Ferriss has control over Camarillo's right arm, including triceps control, which limits Camarillo's ability to pull his elbow back to safety.

b. Ferriss uses his left foot on the hip as a pivot point to push his head closer to Camarillo's knee while his right leg lifts high into the armpit, also pushing Camarillo off balance.

c. From his perpendicular angle, it is easy for Ferriss to hammer his left leg down on Camarillo's head, driving his head to the mat with the armbar locked tight. Camarillo gives way to this motion and allows himself to fall toward his back instead of resisting forward.

d. As Camarillo's left shoulder hits the mat, he straightens his arm, making sure his thumb is pointed toward his crown. Then, he rolls over his left shoulder to escape the armbar. Camarillo continues the escaping movement until he has walked his legs back underneath him.

e. While escaping, Ferriss easily counters by crossing his left leg over Camarillo's shoulder to transition into the omoplata shoulder lock position. Ferriss sits forward and reaches across Camarillo's back to control the position. Camarillo realizes this and pushes off the mat with his left hand to make space for his roll.

f. Camarillo tucks his head underneath his body and lifts his hips skyward.

g. There is nothing left for Camarillo to do except roll! As he rolls, his right leg drives Ferriss's left arm away from the previous body control that he had.

h. As Camarillo lands with his back on the floor, he hugs Ferriss's left hip with his right arm and angles his body to face Ferriss.

i. By angling toward Ferriss, it is far easier for Camarillo to move Ferriss away from him as he bridges his hips into him. This forces Ferriss to fall forward and creates momentum for Camarillo to follow to the top position.

j. Camarillo finishes on the top position and immediately transitions into an over-and-under control to either choke, armlock, or take the back of Ferriss. With this repetition finished, the drill will renew with Ferriss escaping Camarillo's attacks within Camarillo's closed guard.

AFTER-ACTION REPORT:

Lie detection is difficult, but the guerrilla must keep this in the back of his mind while training, drilling, and sparring. It provides an invaluable insight that will allow the guerrilla to control the pace as he decides when he should address a threat as legitimate and when to approach it as weak, half-baked, or as a feint.

Evaluating the threat is one of the most difficult aspects. It is one that can get guerrillas in trouble if done incorrectly, but it can lead to huge gains if successful. Still, this level of Psy-Ops is for those who dare to win.

Victory Belt Publishing Instructional Martial Arts Books

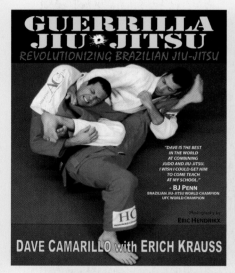

GUERRILLA JIU-JITSU
REVOLUTIONIZING BRAZILIAN JIU-JITSU

"DAVE IS THE BEST IN THE WORLD AT COMBINING JUDO AND JIU-JITSU. I WISH I COULD GET HIM TO COME TEACH AT MY SCHOOL."
- BJ PENN
BRAZILIAN JIU-JITSU WORLD CHAMPION
UFC WORLD CHAMPION

Photography by ERIC HENDRIKX

DAVE CAMARILLO with ERICH KRAUSS

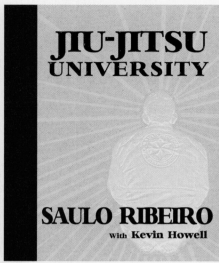

JIU-JITSU UNIVERSITY

SAULO RIBEIRO
with Kevin Howell

ANDRE GALVAO
with Kevin Howell

DRILL TO WIN
12 Months to Better Brazilian Jiu-Jitsu

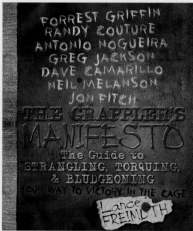

FORREST GRIFFIN
RANDY COUTURE
ANTONIO NOGUEIRA
GREG JACKSON
DAVE CAMARILLO
NEIL MELANSON
JON FITCH

THE GRAPPLER'S MANIFESTO
The Guide to STRANGLING, TORQUING, & BLUDGEONING YOUR WAY TO VICTORY IN THE CAGE

Lance FREIMUTH

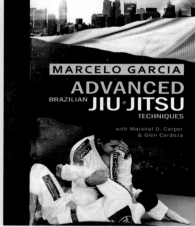

MARCELO GARCIA
ADVANCED
BRAZILIAN **JIU-JITSU** TECHNIQUES

with Marshal D. Carper & Glen Cordoza

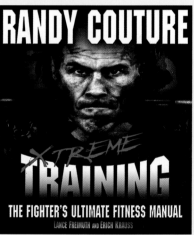

RANDY COUTURE

XTREME TRAINING
THE FIGHTER'S ULTIMATE FITNESS MANUAL
LANCE FREIMUTH and ERICH KRAUSS

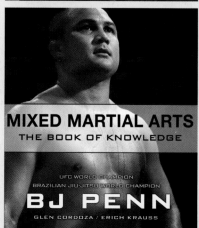

MIXED MARTIAL ARTS
THE BOOK OF KNOWLEDGE

UFC WORLD CHAMPION
BRAZILIAN JIU-JITSU WORLD CHAMPION

BJ PENN

GLEN CORDOZA / ERICH KRAUSS

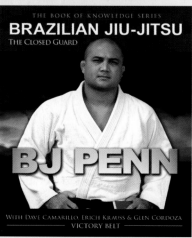

THE BOOK OF KNOWLEDGE SERIES
BRAZILIAN JIU-JITSU
THE CLOSED GUARD

BJ PENN

WITH DAVE CAMARILLO, ERICH KRAUSS & GLEN CORDOZA
VICTORY BELT

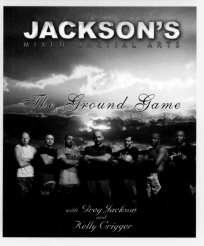

JACKSON'S
MIXED MARTIAL ARTS

The Ground Game

with Greg Jackson and Kelly Crigger

MASTERING
THE TWISTER
JIU JITSU FOR MIXED MARTIAL ARTS COMPETITION

10TH PLANET JIU JITSU

EDDIE BRAVO
with Erich Krauss & Glen Cordoza

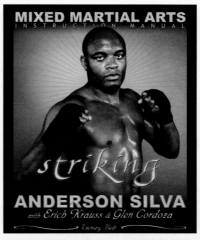

MIXED MARTIAL ARTS
INSTRUCTION MANUAL

striking

ANDERSON SILVA
with Erich Krauss & Glen Cordoza
Victory Belt

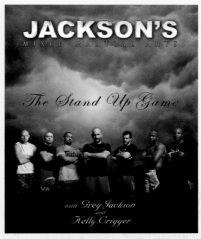

JACKSON'S
MIXED MARTIAL ARTS

The Stand Up Game

with Greg Jackson
and Kelly Crigger

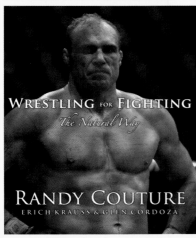

WRESTLING FOR FIGHTING
The Natural Way

RANDY COUTURE
ERICH KRAUSS & GLEN CORDOZA

MASTERING
THE RUBBER GUARD
JIU JITSU FOR MIXED MARTIAL ARTS COMPETITION

10TH PLANET JIU JITSU

EDDIE BRAVO
With Erich Krauss & Glen Cordoza
Foreword by Joe Rogan, Host of NBC's "Fear Factor"

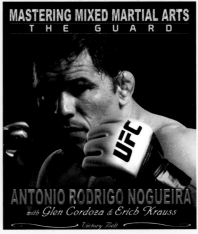

MASTERING MIXED MARTIAL ARTS
THE GUARD

ANTONIO RODRIGO NOGUEIRA
with Glen Cordoza & Erich Krauss
Victory Belt

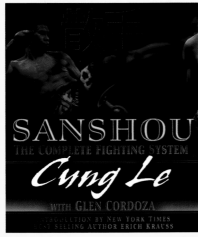

SANSHOU
THE COMPLETE FIGHTING SYSTEM
Cung Le
WITH GLEN CORDOZA
INTRODUCTION BY NEW YORK TIMES
BEST SELLING AUTHOR ERICH KRAUSS

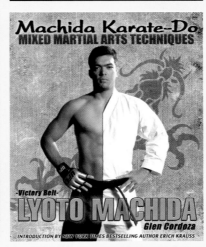

Machida Karate-Do
MIXED MARTIAL ARTS TECHNIQUES

-Victory Belt-
LYOTO MACHIDA
Glen Cordoza
INTRODUCTION BY NEW YORK TIMES BESTSELLING AUTHOR ERICH KRAUSS

Three-time ADCC Submission Wrestling World Champion
MARCELO GARCIA
Five-time Brazilian Jiu-Jitsu World Champion

THE X GUARD

GI & NO GI
JIU-JITSU

Glen Cordoza & Erich Krauss

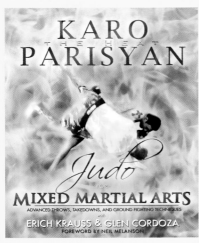

KARO
THE HEAT
PARISYAN

Judo
MIXED MARTIAL ARTS
ADVANCED THROWS, TAKEDOWNS, AND GROUND FIGHTING TECHNIQUES
with
ERICH KRAUSS & GLEN CORDOZA
FOREWORD BY NEIL MELANSON

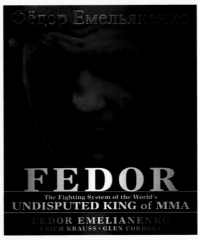

Фёдор Емельяненко

FEDOR
The Fighting System of the World's
UNDISPUTED KING of MMA
FEDOR EMELIANENKO
ERICH KRAUSS & GLEN CORDOZA

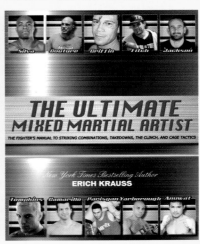

THE ULTIMATE
MIXED MARTIAL ARTIST
THE FIGHTER'S MANUAL TO STRIKING COMBINATIONS, TAKEDOWNS, THE CLINCH, AND CAGE TACTICS

New York Times Bestselling Author
ERICH KRAUSS

ABOUT THE AUTHORS

Dave Camarillo *is a judo and jiu-jitsu black belt that has combined both arts at the highest levels to create the Guerrilla Jiu-Jitsu system. Once lauded by Rickson Gracie as the "Most Technical American Jiu-Jitsu Fighter" and having reached the number two national ranking in judo, Dave now focuses his attention on creating champions at his Guerrilla Jiu-Jitsu academies in Pleasanton and San Jose, California, where he teaches everyone from world champions and UFC belt holders to hobbyists and martial arts enthusiasts. He is the author of* Guerrilla Jiu-Jitsu: Revolutionizing Brazilian Jiu-Jitsu.

Kevin Howell *is an author and former political science professor based out of Long Beach, California. His love for jiu-jitsu and judo combined with his academic sensibilities have led to a promising writing career as showcased by his two best selling books,* Jiu-Jitsu University *and* Drill to Win. *When he isn't writing, Kevin shares his unique jiu-jitsu and grappling experiences with his students at The Jiu-Jitsu League in Long Beach, California.*